The

Awakening

of a

Surgeon

A FAMILY GUIDE TO PREVENTING
SPORTS INJURIES AND DEATH

David H. Janda, MD

D1502106

David H. Janda, MD
The Michigan Orthopaedic Center
5315 Elliott Dr.
Suite 301
Ypsilanti, MI 48197

Printed and bound in the U.S.A.

10 9 8 7 6 5 4 3 2

Library of Congress Cataloging-in-Publication Data on file.
ISBN: 0-9745655-1-2

Dave,
Dream Big!
Dave J.

This book is dedicated to my parents, Ben and Ruth Janda,
my wife, Libby, and our children Allison and Katie.
My parents taught me to keep my feet on the ground
and reach for the stars. I have had the fortunate opportunity
to grasp onto three shining stars—my wife, and my two daughters.

by train. Out the windows we drink in the passing scene of cars on the nearby highway, of children waving at the crossing, of cattle grazing at a distant hillside, of smoke pouring from a power plant, of row upon row of corn and wheat, of flatlands and valleys, of mountains and rolling hillsides, of city skylights and village halls.

But uppermost in our minds is the final destination. On a certain day, at a certain hour we will pull into the station. Bands will be playing and flags waving. Once we get there so many wonderful dreams will come true, and the pieces of our lives will fit together like a completed jigsaw puzzle. How restlessly we pace the aisles, damning the minutes for loitering—waiting, waiting, waiting for the station.

"When we reach the station, that will be it!" we cry. "When I am eighteen." "When I buy a new 450SL Mercedes Benz!" "When I put the last kid through college." "When I have paid off the mortgage!" "When I get a promotion." "When I reach the age of retirement, I shall live happily ever after!"

Sooner or later we must realize there is no station, no one place to arrive at once and for all. The true joy of life is the trip. The station is only a dream. It constantly outdistances us.

"Relish the moment" is a good motto, especially when coupled with Psalm 1-18:24 'This is the day which the Lord hath made; we will rejoice and be glad in it.' It isn't the burdens of today that drive men mad. It is the regrets over yesterday and the fear of tomorrow. Regret and fear are twin thieves who rob us of today.

So, stop pacing the aisles and counting the miles. Instead climb more mountains, eat more ice cream, go barefoot more often, swim more rivers, watch more sunsets, laugh more, cry less. Life must be lived as we go along. The station will come soon enough.

Hopefully, at the end of *The Awakening of a Surgeon*, you will be inspired to travel on your own journey by *Dreaming Big and Daring to Fail!*

CHAPTER ONE

The Awakening

"God Himself does not speak prose, but communicates with us by hints, omens, inference and dark resemblances in objects lying all around us."

—Ralph Waldo Emerson,
"Poetry in Imagination," Letters and Social Aims.

Chicago, July 28, 1989

It was one of those dog days when the heat seems to rise in waves over you. I lay in the backseat of my dad's new Deville enveloped in a suffocating shroud of stale, still air. The sweat clung to my skin like soot. A blast from the air-conditioner hit me flush and sent a shiver down my spine. I pulled on my sweater and wrapped myself in a blanket. Then I huddled in a corner. I felt parched, feverish, and chilly all at the same time. Though my health mattered, my thoughts were completely consumed by my 11-month-old daughter Allison and her bone marrow results.

The fever made my head spin as I lost my thought in a fog. I couldn't concentrate. I thought I was a kid again, sitting in the backseat of my dad's old Chevy traveling through the Mojave

Desert for mile after barren mile of miserable mind-numbing heat and blistering sun. It was our summer vacation, and the Chevy, with its broken down air-conditioner and vinyl seats that pinched me and peeled my skin, was the kind of car Dad drove all his life before giving himself the Deville on his retirement.

I shivered again and wrapped the blanket tighter. Nobody spoke and the silence seemed strange. Dad and Mom always talked on our trips. Mom, a retired history teacher, regaled us with her updates on world events, while Dad, the former president of a large construction company, spoke untiringly about the stock market, and business, and sports. They were great conversationalists. But now none of us said a word. Even the radio remained eerily silent.

Until a moment like this hits, you forget how the illness of one's child can put things in perspective. Just a few days previously, my wife Libby and I sat in our living room planning our family celebration on Mackinac Island as we looked at photos from our last trip there. But now all our energies were focused on getting Allison through today, our family through today, and everything rested on that single purpose.

I recalled the veranda of the Grand Hotel, a dominating, white, century-old building looking out over the Straits of Mackinac. It was an elegant place and a step back in time—a resting place. And after four years of medical school and five years of orthopedic residency, I needed a rest. The plan was for my parents and aunts to join Libby, Allison, and me in Mackinac, following my Board examination in Chicago.

We had planned this family vacation to celebrate the end of my residency and the completion of my Boards. This was the culmination of my medical training. Everything that I had worked for was on the line. If I passed my Board examination, I would become a full-fledged orthopedic surgeon and begin the practice to which I had devoted my life.

But everything came to a screeching halt. The day I left Ann Arbor, I wasn't feeling well. My head ached and my throat felt raspy. I thought I had a touch of the flu, but I couldn't let that stop me now, not after 5 years of intense, grueling study. I had to complete my Boards. And so I rushed to the airport and caught the flight to Chicago. As I sat in the plane, I felt guilty about leaving. Allison seemed to have caught the same bug and I was concerned. I planned to call home as soon as I arrived in Chicago.

By the time I got to my hotel, things had gone from bad to worse. My raspy throat had become inflamed, and my body ached and burned. I knew it was going to be a struggle to take the Boards. Even more worrisome, I found a message in my hotel room. "Call Libby." Now if you knew Libby, you'd know this was a cause for concern. Maybe it's her Pennsylvania Dutch upbringing, but she never calls unless it's very important.

"Something's wrong," echoed through my entire body as I dialed home.

Libby answered the phone on the first ring. "Dave," she said. "It's Allison. She has a temperature of 104. Dr. Graves asked me to bring her in for a blood test and he's considering admitting her to the hospital." A chill ran through me. I sat down on the bed, feeling helpless not being there.

Now Bill Graves is as cool as a cucumber. Some doctors try to prepare their patients for any outcome by telling them the worse that can happen. I don't share this philosophy and neither does Bill. I knew that for him to say he was considering admitting her to the hospital meant there was a cause for alarm. Libby told me that Bill wanted to see Allison again in the morning just when I would be taking my Boards. I resolved to leave for Ann Arbor immediately after my exam.

Between the worrying about Allison and the fever, I only slept in fits and starts. By the next morning, I had a high fever, chills, and the shakes. My mouth felt like a coke oven and I could barely swallow. I slowly rolled out of bed, dressed and threw on a sweater. I staggered down to the basement of the Hyatt, a large cinderblock warehouse of a room filled with rows of folding tables. I sat down and waited. I almost didn't even notice as the others sat down around me; it was a bit like I was watching from outside my body. The proctor passed out the tests and I began.

Despite my fever and the fact that the room was 85 degrees, I continued to shiver and kept my sweater on throughout the exam. I sat in that room shivering and shaking through six hours of that grueling test without taking a break. We couldn't even go to the bathroom without the proctor accompanying us. Finally, exhausted and spent, I finished. I thought I had failed the test and I didn't care. I put my pencil down and now focused on getting home.

John Lane, a good friend of mine who took the test with me, told me that he planned to drive back to Ann Arbor immediately after the exam. He agreed to look in on Allison for me. John, a tall and athletic looking laid-back surfer with dishwater blond streaked hair, grew up in Hollywood where he went to Hollywood High. He played minor league baseball, but chose medical school over the majors. I met John during our residency and we became close. He was like my brother and practically lived at our house. At any rate, John left as planned and drove back to Ann Arbor with his girlfriend Allison Sundberg, after whom my daughter was named. I was in no condition to travel back to Ann Arbor, so my dad picked me up and drove me to our home in Western Springs about 30 minutes outside of Chicago.

It wasn't an accident I chose to stay with them. I think probably the best way to describe my relationship with my parents is as very close friends. They've been my guidance counselors. They are there for me when good things happen and more importantly, they are there when things don't go well. When as a kid I was one of the finalists for the Westinghouse Science Talent Search in Washington, one of the interviewers asked me about family relationships. I told him, and I still feel to this day that I consider my parents and my entire family among my best friends.

After I settled into my room at my parent's house, I called Libby. No one was home. I lay in bed nervously waiting for her call. My flu continued to get worse and by the time the phone rang two hours later, I could barely crawl out of bed.

"Hello, Libby," I croaked in a hoarse, pinched voice. "How's Allison?"

"Dr. Graves says she has an abnormal white blood cell count."

We were both quiet. My mind raced without any words coming out. That could mean only two things. Either the virus had suppressed Allison's bone marrow count, or she had leukemia. The suggestion that she might have leukemia threw out all thoughts about how I had done on the Boards or my own fever. "I'm leaving now."

"You sound worse, leave tomorrow. One of us in the hospital is enough. We need to focus and plan for Allison. Do not come home. I will call."

Libby promised to call later that night. I hung up and waited, more anxious than ever. The phone rang again around 11 p.m. Allison had been admitted to Mott's Children's Hospital, and Dr. Graves planned to perform a bone marrow examination in the early morning. I was thankful to hear that John Lane and Allison Sundberg had arrived and stayed with Libby and Allison while she was admitted. Libby and I agreed that my folks and I would return that morning. "I'm leaving now."

"No, you're not. Rest, leave early, let the other doctors do their work."

None of us slept that night, not my dad or mom or me. We

were exhausted by the time we left Chicago at 5:00 a.m. The chills and fever stayed with me the entire way.

We arrived at the hospital four hours later that morning. My mom and dad ran up to Allison's floor. I struggled along after them going only on fear and adrenaline. Dr. Graves had just finished taking Allison's bone marrow and she was extremely lethargic, and not responding at all. I put my arms around Libby. She gripped me tighter than ever before. She's always upbeat and perky, but now she seemed tired and worn-out. She hadn't slept much and her eyes were red. Her always well-kept hair looked disheveled. No one said much of anything; we were all in a state of panic and fear.

An hour or so later, Libby and my mom left for home to get some rest. Now it was my turn to give her a rest and I told her to leave, thankful for how she had gotten us to this point. Dad and I remained with Allison. What happened then—well, it's difficult to explain, but it happened. I lifted Allison out of her bed, a kind of elevated crib. She didn't respond. Before her illness, her bright blue eyes used to sparkle and flash and she was always chirping, squealing, and giggling. One of the things she used to like to do before she became ill was to tease me. I'd try to get her to say, "Daddy" and she'd get this little sparkle in her eyes and look at me and say, "Momma." But as I held her now she laid in my arms limp, white as a ghost, her eyes closed and unresponsive. I noticed the IV in her hand. At that point I said a prayer, I told God I would gladly change places with Allison, and asked Him to take me, not Allison. I prayed that this wasn't leukemia.

As I was saying this prayer, I heard a still, soft voice whisper to me. The closest I can describe it is like the voice that Kevin Costner keeps hearing in the movie "Field of Dreams." The voice whispered, "Don't stop your research. Establish an institute. Focus on prevention."

I thought maybe my dad had spoken. I opened my eyes, and looked over to him.

"Did you say something to me?" I asked.

"No," he responded. "Why?"

"Did you say something to me about research or prevention and an institute?"

"No!" he said and looked at me strangely, wondering about my fever.

I closed my eyes, and kept saying a prayer. I didn't hear anything more, but I lowered my head and whispered to the voice, "I will continue my research. I will continue the prevention research, and I will establish a research institute. Just take care of Allison."

I finished the prayer and opened my eyes. I looked down at Allison. Several minutes later, she opened her eyes, and looked up at me and said "Momma." The sparkle was back and she started to chirp and squeal again. About 15 minutes later, the doctors returned. They announced that she had a viral suppression of her bone marrow. But I already knew she was okay . . . my prayer was answered; she didn't have leukemia.

This was one of the most important and happiest moments in my life—right up there with my marriage to Libby and the birth of Allison and our younger daughter Katie. I felt incredibly elated, relieved, and thankful. We had dodged the worst fear a parent can have—the sickness and potential death of their child.

I don't consider myself a deeply religious person. I don't think anyone who knows me would accuse me of wearing my religion on my sleeve. On the other hand, I do have a deep faith in God. As a physician, the more you take care of people, the more you realize there is a higher power. All you can do as a physician is temporize life; you cannot control it. A much larger and greater force calls the shots. As a physician, you can have a say and make an impact in a patient's life, but needless to say, you don't have the last word on the subject.

The experience gave me new meaning for the words of former Supreme Court Justice William O. Douglas, "Men may believe what they cannot prove. . . . Religious experiences which are as real as life to some may be incomprehensible to others."

One month later, my consuming thought was to never see Allison sick again, to never have the empty feeling inside, to make good on my deal, to establish the Institute for Preventive Sports Medicine. Over the past 11 years since that seeringly hot day in July, many people have asked me: "Why do you put in all the time and effort? Why do you put up with all the threats and all the problems raising money? Why do you spend an extra 20 hours a week, every week, for 11 years, working on the Institute when you haven't received a penny's pay for it? Why do you do it?"

My answer has always been, "Because I enjoy it. It's a hobby. It takes the place of golf." But the truth is that on that day in July, I cut a deal with a much higher power and as far as I am concerned, I owe that higher power my daughter's life. That's the reason why I spend the extra time, the reason why I push as hard as I push, the reason why, if someone stands in my way, I try to go around them, and if I'm unable to go around them, I go through them.

I made a commitment, a deal, to establish an Institute, to follow through on my research. I believe if I stopped, I would have broken the bond, the trust, and the commitment I made on that incredible day in July.

CHAPTER TWO

A Simple Observation

"Thousands upon thousands of persons have studied disease. Almost no one has studied health."

—ADELLE DAVIS

My odyssey in prevention began five years before that fateful day in July. I began my orthopedic residency at the University of Michigan in the fall of 1984. It was here during an emergency room stint that I first saw the injuries which became the foundation of our research at the Institute.

Residency is an extremely difficult time for physicians. During the first two years, you're on call every other night. You work around-the-clock rotations, 40 hours on with almost no sleep and eight hours off if you're lucky. Most of our work involved taking care of patients' needs in their rooms, commonly called "scut." Nobody wants to do it. Only on rare occasions would you actually spend time in the operating room. Typically, you would take about 30 calls an hour from a nurse about setting lines for patients: central lines, IVs, chest tubes, blood drains, nasogastric tubes, and feeding lines. Sometimes the calls involved talking to families, managing fluids, looking up labs, writing daily notes, or completing insurance forms. The floor work took hours and hours. You usually complete the "scut" around 7:00 to 8:00 p.m., and then started rounds seeing all the patients on the service and reviewing their charts. This took, on average, about two hours. You would go home at about 11:00 p.m., only to return the next morning at 5:00 a.m.

This schedule was not conducive to family life, or to having a life, period. Sometimes you don't go home for four or five days in a row, and when you do go home, you're so tired you can barely keep your head straight. You're not exactly the best conversationalist to have around. Libby and I had just married and it's amazing our marriage survived the ordeal—a fact that I attribute only to her patience and understanding. I was very fortunate to have her there as my support. It takes a very special person to live with a physician or a nurse or a therapist, or anyone involved in the medical profession. All too often, circumstances and patient predicaments take precedent over family and friends. You essentially lose your life in service to others and your loved ones really lose pieces of you because of circumstances—circumstances that especially during residency prove to be brutal (particularly in the first two years). Besides the unreal hours, you receive poor treatment from the faculty and even the older residents. Essentially, you are their slave.

On top of all this, the University of Michigan, where I trained, required orthpedic surgery residents to spend two years in general surgery before beginning their three years in orthopedics. All other orthopedic residency programs in the U.S. (except Duke University) had moved to one year of general surgery, and four years of orthopedic surgery.

When you're training to be an orthopedic surgeon, spending time in general surgery allows some advantages. A general surgery internship develops your surgical judgment and gives you a broader, whole-body approach to treating surgical problems. However, we spent two years in servitude in general surgery and that's overkill. Those of us who wanted to practice as orthopedic surgeons found it very frustrating spending two years under the direction of general surgeons, dealing with head injuries, gastrointestinal problems, and cardiac cases—conditions that we knew we would never treat again. We were chomping at the bit to enter our chosen field and begin developing the skills we knew we would need in our practice.

Residency also proved frustrating because you know the clock is ticking and you're not moving ahead in your chosen field. Furthermore, you're still in training, having completed four years of college and four years of medical school, while your friends have completed school and are earning a living. So, residency is a very brutal and frustrating time and it's not long before you begin to have discussions with yourself and other residents about whether you have made the right decision.

I recall one occasion in particular, during our second month of residency, when six of my orthopedic surgery classmates and I got together to commiserate about our lot. It was about 3:00 a.m. and we sat on the floor in a darkened hallway, complaining that being a resident was rather like being a prisoner of war. All of us were feeling broken down, beaten up, like we didn't have anything left to give.

It just happened that during the second month of residency, one resident dropped out of the program. This opened up a hole and I was placed in the emergency room well ahead of my training schedule. Normally you don't do the emergency room rotation until you're in your second year. So I soon found myself serving as the trauma coordinator in the emergency room, and the sole surgeon evaluating every trauma case and every surgery-related problem. I'd look at every patient and contact the appropriate service for his/her treatment program.

In a 24-hour period, I would see dozens and dozens of patients. It was extremely busy and actually pretty scary, because there I was, two months out of medical school and I'm in charge of all the major trauma cases coming in the emergency room, as well as many general surgery cases and vascular surgery cases. It seemed like I was Mark Green of ER when I only had the knowledge of John Carter—I was in the position of Dr. Hawkeye Pierce of MASH when my knowledge was that of Corporal Max Klinger.

Two events happened that month that will give you an idea what it was like. One day, the emergency and trauma services helicopter transported an older gentleman, a smoker with emphysema, cardiac disease, and one kidney, to the emergency room. The hospital transferring him to our emergency room said that he had a large aortic aneurysm, a ballooning of the aorta (the large artery coming out of the heart), on the verge of rupturing. While in flight, the aneurysm did rupture. By the time the paramedics brought him into the emergency room, essentially, he had died. But we didn't give up. Another resident and I gave him CPR and revived him. Then we called the attending vascular staff, rushed the gentleman up to the operating room, and started operating on him. We were 15 minutes into the operation when the staff showed up and finished. We were amazed that the patient lived and actually left the hospital within seven to ten days. It was an enormous feeling of success, so much so that I knew that maybe I could make it through this phase of training. As a minor complication, the patient suffered two days of diarrhea during his post-operative hospital stay. Several months later I was served with a subpoena asking me to show up in court. The elderly gentleman decided to sue all of us involved in his care for malpractice. Even though he was dead when he arrived, and we saved his life and he ended up walking out of the hospital in under 10 days, he sued us because he suffered two days of diarrhea. Such is the lot of physicians in these litigious times.

The other event proved much more tragic. The resident working on the 24-hour shift opposite me had been dating a secretary on another hospital floor. He had just split up with her and she showed up one night in the emergency room parking lot with a gun. Security guards tried to talk her out of hurting herself, but their attempts proved unsuccessful. She shot herself and died on the spot, an incredibly tragic event. After her death, her extremely distraught former boyfriend didn't return to work for a week. As a result, I worked every night rather than every other night for the entire week. I'd work 24 hours, go home for about six hours to get some sleep, and return for another 24-hour shift.

So, I spent one long stretch in the emergency room. Now my dad always said that, "When you're handed a bad deal in life and a gross of lemons, rather than gripe and moan, the best thing is to make lemonade." So that's what I did. During the extra time I spent in the hospital, I began to do a little research on the injuries that I saw in the emergency room. Surprisingly, I found that almost half the folks came in with sports injuries and, in particular, softball injuries. I looked at the records and found that most of these injuries appeared to occur when players slid into bases. I found all this very interesting and took the records to one of the orthopedic staff at the University of Michigan, Dr. Fred Hankin. If I had spoken to anyone but Fred, the matter probably wouldn't have gone any further. Most of the medical staff wouldn't bother to spend the time talking to a resident about his clinical findings. But Fred was different. A big teddy bear of a man, he was a resident education advocate and really wanted the residents to enjoy and learn while doing their time at the University as best as they could. He had completed the residency program not long before we had arrived and understood what we were going through. I found in him a willing advocate and collaborator.

So I showed the records to Fred and told him about my findings. He told me that he, too, had seen many cases of folks injured playing softball and most of these injuries seemed to occur sliding into bases. What's more, he had operated on several patients with sliding injuries and many were serious—not just sprains, but wrist fractures, ankle fractures, and elbow dislocations. So Fred suggested that we review the emergency room records of people injured while playing softball in the Ann Arbor community and in the intramural leagues at the University of Michigan over a two-year time period to see what we could find.

So everyday after the emergency room settled down, usually between 3:00 and 5:00 a.m., I poured through the records. You can sleep some from 3:00 and 5:00 a.m., but by the time you wake up, you feel hung over. So, I figured why not just spend the time reviewing the records and get the work done while I was still at the hospital? And that's what I did. Throughout my month in the emergency room, from 3:00 to 5:00 a.m. and whenever there was a lull in the action, I would fight the urge to sleep that your body is literally demanding and I reviewed the records. I compiled the data and the results were startling. I found that approximately three-quarters of all softball injuries in the Ann Arbor community resulted from sliding into bases. I brought these findings to Fred. When he saw the results in black and white, it became crystal clear and confirmed my earlier suspicions. He reviewed my research and suggested that I put my findings in writing. So I began to put pen to paper during that 3:00 to 5:00 a.m. lull. And every other day Fred would review my results.

There were individuals in academic medicine who place their name on studies conducted by their residents even though they put little, if any, effort into the study. Fred was truly an exception to the rule. He reviewed the study at every stage. He went through every section with me, helped rewrite it, and proved extremely helpful in bringing the study to its written conclusion. His efforts literally saved years in getting the information to the public.

So, in spite of all the flurry of activity and chaos going on in the emergency room, such as opening up people's abdomens for bleeding aneurysms and the shooting incident with the young lady that led to my working almost a week without a day off, we completed the study. Fred suggested we submit it for publication. I agreed and we prepared the manuscript. We included with our data an argument for a prevention approach to the problem, suggesting several measures for preventing sliding injuries.

We first submitted the study to a prestigious sports medicine journal. The editor rejected it outright. He said that a study of this nature would benefit no one and provided no insight into sports medicine because, as he expressed it, "prevention doesn't have very much to do with the issue of sports medicine."

In essence, the study was rejected because we had a different approach to sports medicine research. The vast majority of studies appearing in sports medicine journals at that time had focused on dozens of different ways to reconstruct a ligament. I believe that if you already have 10 good ways to reconstruct a ligament, why do you need 11, 12, 13, or 43 more ways? So at that point most sports medicine studies looked at injuries and treatment and didn't go the next step of recognizing injury patterns and look at ways to prevent such patterns from reoccurring. That's what our study did.

Nevertheless, I found the rejection very discouraging. Fred, a veteran in the medical publishing world, reassured me. "It's alright," he said. "I've been rejected before and I'll be rejected again, and so will you. Let's go to a different journal." And we did.

We submitted the study to the *American Journal of Family Physicians,* and, actually, this probably was a better choice since the vast majority of physicians that read this journal treat weekend warriors rather than the professional and other high performance athletes treated by most readers of sports medicine journals. The family physician journal accepted our study without hesitation, and published it immediately. So the selfdoubt I had from being rejected was now instantly replaced with conviction—our work was important and did have a vision, a purpose.

This small initial step became the foundation for The Institute for Preventative Sports Medicine. The study, its findings, and the recommendations for further research that we outlined in the study became the basis for all our future prevention efforts. All that transpired thereafter came from that very simple observation in the emergency room, i.e., that a significant number of folks came in with injuries that suggested a pattern. This particular injury pattern related to softball and, in particular, sliding into a fixed, immovable object—the stationary base found on all the recreational fields in Ann Arbor, and every other town and city across America.

Throughout my residency, we continued to look at ways to reduce and prevent these injuries. We explored many avenues and came to several dead ends before we hit on a solution that the Center for Disease Control concluded could lead to the prevention of 1.7 million injuries a year in the United States and save two billion dollars in health care costs a year.

CHAPTER THREE

The Killing Fields

"Baseball is not unlike a war."

—TY COBB

They call them the killing fields. Rocky, sunbaked, hard as concrete, pothole-filled battlefields—that's what the softball players in Ann Arbor and across the country play on, not the well-kept, manicured, grass fields on which the pros play. They're injuries waiting to happen. And, unfortunately, injuries do happen all too regularly. It's a story common to recreational athletes playing on community fields throughout the U.S. Poorly conditioned players play on poor fields using poor sliding techniques. The result is over two million injuries a year in the U.S. These include bruises, contusions, lacerations, sprains and strains, all the typical injuries you would expect. But when we began our softball sliding studies, I saw players come in to the University of Michigan emergency room with much worse: ankle fractures, knee sprains, wrist and shoulder dislocations, even head injuries (from sliding head first and missing the bag with their hand).

One day a player came in with an ankle dislocation so severe his ankle had twisted off the foot bone. The injury was severe enough, but there also was a good chance it would become infected. I told the player and his wife that if the ankle did become infected, he would need an amputation. He was very lucky. It didn't come to this, and six months after surgery he was back jogging two miles every other day. The surgery proved successful, but it wasn't over for him. He was a salesman and lost half a year's salary because he could not get back on his feet to travel for several months. Furthermore, it's highly likely he will develop a degenerative condition in the ankle that will lead to significantly more medical costs down the road. After I treated him, I began to realize why the players called them the killing fields.

I continued to see many such players over the next two years as we followed up on our initial study of sliding injuries. We spoke about their injuries and how they occurred and how they might have been prevented. Based on these discussions and our research, Dr. Hankin and I began to discuss potential means of reducing softball injuries in our community. We had already identified sliding as the cause for most of these injuries. So our first thought simply was to ask the leagues to abolish sliding. But I had played baseball for years; I loved the game as most young kids did in the '70s. We blindly and naively thought it was a no-brainer. We took our abolishing sliding idea to the killing fields and spoke directly with the players. At one of their meetings we had 25 players, representatives of each team in the league. We spoke with them about the high emotional, physical, and economical costs of these kinds of injuries. We told them we wanted to find a way to reduce, if not eliminate sliding injuries and how we thought abolishing sliding would accomplish this. Our effort proved an abysmal failure. Some called me Lenin—not John Lennon, but V.I. Lenin or at least Lenin's grandson, a Communist trying to ruin the national pastime, and I can imagine how they saw me, a physician trying to tell them how to play their game.

After some laughing and smiling, more restrained players and league officials told us that sliding was an integral part of the game, and that if we attempted to introduce a no-sliding rule into the leagues, players would just pick up and move to a league that did allow sliding. Frustrated and deflated, we needed to rethink our strategy. So we decided to speak with the director of the intramural softball and baseball leagues at the University of Michigan, Moby Benedict. Truly a legend at the University of Michigan, Moby coached the varsity men's baseball team for over 30 years and became one of the NCAA's winningest coaches of all times. His teams produced many professional athletes. Even more important, Moby became known and continues to be known as one of the most sincere, honest, and straightforward individuals involved in the sports of baseball and softball. The University named their baseball field after him.

We spoke with Moby about our findings and he told us he wasn't surprised. He knew the dangers of sliding improperly and, while serving as the University's men's baseball coach, had stressed the techniques of proper sliding. Furthermore, he conducted many sliding seminars for his players to teach them how to prevent injury, far ahead of his time at that level. We thought this might be a more promising approach and with the help of local physicians at the University of Michigan, Dr. Ed Wojtys and Dr. Gerald O'Connor, Dr. Hankin and I developed a series of seminars to teach players the technique of proper sliding.

We held the seminars at the university and 50 or so weekend athletes attended. Unfortunately, this number proved quite low compared to the much greater numbers playing softball and baseball in our community. Consequently, we saw no reduction in sliding injuries as a result of our efforts.

So basically, we had two strikes on us and we were batting zero. At this point, we decided that if we couldn't abolish sliding and we couldn't teach players the appropriate sliding techniques, the only other option would be to use safer equipment, and specifically a safer alternative to the base into which players slid.

The standard, stationary base used in softball and baseball at all levels looks like a little white pillow. Looks are deceiving and I think stationary bases might more appropriately be compared to an iceberg. The player sliding into that iceberg is the Titanic. That little white pillow is bolted to a metal post, then sunk into the ground, and fixed in concrete. It takes a tremendous amount of force to break a stationary base from its moorings, about 3,500 foot-pounds. To date, I have never seen or heard of one ever breaking off the post. So a player who slides into this iceberg the wrong way can do a tremendous amount of damage to him or herself.

Dr. Hankin and I started looking at other types of bases that might be less dangerous. At first, we said let's make the bases all flush to the infield surface. You can use recessed bases in the infield just like you use for home plate. You see few injuries from sliding into home plate. Here we ran into another problem. On recreational fields, you only have one umpire. There's no umpire at second or third, so it's difficult to see a recessed base and call the slide safe or out. That solution wouldn't work.

So we decided to contact city recreation departments and ask for players' experiences with alternative base systems. With Moby Benedict's help, we contacted many officials in recreational departments throughout the U.S. Some people told us about Velcro breakaway bases and magnetic breakaway bases. We asked about players' experiences with both and neither type seemed satisfactory. In fact, they actually seemed to cause more injuries. They became unstable as dirt and water got between the bases and altered how they broke away. We had just about given up hope

when, finally, through a circuitous route, I discovered league officials in Tucson, Arizona who had a limited experience with a
more promising type of breakaway base. This base consisted of
two major parts: a rubber mat with a post inserted into the ground
like a stationary base, and a separate pillow-like base that snapped
over it. The mat had rubber thumbs or grommets that stuck out
from the top; the base had receiving holes on one side that
snapped over the grommets. The two pieces essentially snapped
together like Legos and separated when a player slid into the base
with sufficient force. From the field, you couldn't tell the difference between a breakaway base and a standard stationary base.

This breakaway base included a youth model, a teen model,
an adult model, and a pro model. They differed only in the
amount of force it took to pop the white pillow from the rest of
the base. Despite the fact that the people in Tucson had very limited experience with the bases, less than a year, they felt that players sustained fewer injuries on them. However, they had no data
to compare them with stationary bases. I asked where I could
obtain some of these bases. They referred me to the Hollywood
Base Company, an outfit marketing the bases in California.

The Hollywood Base Company is one of the largest suppliers
of stationary bases in the world and they held the marketing and
distribution rights for a breakaway base. I called the company and
spoke to a sales representative, Rick Porter. He told me that Roger
Hall, a college baseball coach from Elizabethtown, Pennsylvania
had invented the base 13 or 14 years previously. He had approached several individuals and organizations about testing the
base, but no university and no one in the field of sports medicine
seemed interested in a study looking at the prevention of sliding
injuries.

I told Mr. Porter that if the company could supply me with
some of the bases, we would do everything we could to get them

placed on the University of Michigan intramural fields and institute a study comparing injuries on them with injuries on the standard, stationary base. He was enthusiastic. He told me he had been involved in the baseball community as a sales rep for several years and knew that stationary bases caused injuries. He wanted to help us and agreed to supply us with Roger's bases for our study.

So we had our bases and were ready to begin our study. That's when we came across our next stumbling block. The players and the coaches had agreed to cooperate in the study. Moby Benedict had agreed to participate, as the director of the university's intramural softball program. The director of intramural sports at the university, Dr. Mike Stevenson, felt that this study was long overdue, and enthusiastically supported participating in the study. So he came on board and it was all systems go—or so we thought. I made some preliminary calls to the athletic department to get a clearance for us to change over half of the university's fields to breakaway bases. I received no response for weeks on end. Unfortunately, the athletic powers that be did not want to get involved in a "medical" study, and essentially kept putting us off. They wouldn't give us the go-ahead.

We had willing participants on the fields. We had willing administration on the fields. We had field supervisors, members of the research team who agreed to monitor games and record the number of slides and injuries. But we couldn't get the go-ahead from the athletic department administrators who, unfortunately, like many hospital and HMO administrators, don't care to spend time on the front lines. We make fun of the fact that we never see a hospital administrator in the emergency room, in the operating room, on the floors, or on the wards, where you find patients.

Dr. Wojtys spoke to Moby about the administration's lack of response, and he said he doubted the athletic department would ever give us a positive response. I was concerned we'd never get the study off the ground. So I sat down with Moby, and we discussed various options. I said that players were getting injured needlessly like the one who dislocated his ankle so severely that he had twisted his ankle off the foot bone and required major surgery on it and would have lost his foot if any infection had set in. I was getting frustrated that no one was doing anything about injuries like this. "Don't sweat it," he said. Moby's the original "don't sweat the small stuff" kind of guy. He gave one of his gap-toothed grins and said, "We'll get this thing going. Don't let it bug you. We'll do what's right for folks." And without hesitating, he suggested that we take the initiative without waiting for the administration's approval. I knew pursuing this was an enormous act of courage, to do what was right for people at the expense of his job—and he was so nonchalant about it. "Let's switch half of the fields over to breakaways," Moby said. "They'll never know if we do or don't do this study. The players need it, so let's do it." As far as he was concerned, if the players agreed to participate in the study, that was all the approval we needed. Fortunately, Dr. Stevenson agreed.

And that's how we got started. I owe a big debt to Moby. It's individuals like him and Dr. Mike Stevenson who truly have been the major players in our research. Without their help and assistance, the study never would have gotten off the ground.

We installed the breakaway bases on six fields and the standard stationary bases on six fields. Then we put together our research team. We enlisted the support of field supervisors and emergency room nurses at the University Hospital and St. Joseph's Mercy Hospital. We're fortunate that Ann Arbor is a small enough community that we have only two hospitals. Furthermore, the community had experience with medical tracking studies, having participated in cardiac, pulmonary, and infectious disease tracking studies. We also enlisted the help of the nurses in the student health service. So when players injured themselves sliding on our study fields, our field supervisors recorded it, and if they happened to miss an injury, we picked it up through one of the emergency rooms, through the student health service and through private practitioners in town recording injuries—a logistics nightmare, but crucial in getting it right.

When players injured themselves on our study fields, I contacted them and brought them in to the orthopedic clinic or the student health service for treatment. If a private practitioner saw the injured player, I followed up, contacting the athlete by phone and asking for a copy of his or her medical records. We also asked them to keep track over the next year of the medical costs associated with the injury they sustained.

Before we began the study, we heard some concerns expressed that the breakaway bases might stop the action and slow down play or that a base popping off might make it difficult to call a player safe or out. We watched for this, but, in fact, it never happened. Bases did pop off, but when that occurred, the bottom part, the stationary mat that lies flush with the infield surface, remained behind as the base. "Lost" time was 15 seconds, considerably less time than that spent in attending to a player injured on the field from sliding into a stationary base.

So on both counts, we had no complaints and experienced no problems with the bases over the two-year time frame of the study. In two years we had no word at all from the administration. During this time, teams played 637 games on the breakaway-base fields and 635 on stationary-base fields. The same players in the same leagues played in all the games. By the end of the study, 45 people sustained injuries on the stationary-base fields, and two on the breakaway-base fields. In other words, we realized a 96% reduction in injuries by switching from stationary bases to breakaway bases. Furthermore, the 45 people injured on the stationary bases had medical bills of over $50,000 during a one-year period.

The two people injured on the breakaway bases had medical bills of $700. So we also experienced a 99% reduction in health care expenditures by switching from stationary to breakaway bases. Furthermore, we found that, on an average, injured players missed about 14 days of work due to their injury. In some cases, this cost could be incredibly expensive; e.g., the salesman with the dislocated ankle I spoke about earlier that lost half a year's salary because he could not get back on his feet to travel.

I compiled the data and reviewed it with Dr. Hankin, Dr. Wojtys, and Moby Benedict. We integrated some of the field supervisors' experiences with the bases into the study; e.g., how well the players accepted the bases, whether there were any problems with "safe" versus "out" calls, and whether there were any delays of games. I wrote the study and Dr. Hankin and Dr. Wojtys edited it. Not surprisingly, we concluded that, based on our experience, fields should be switched over from stationary to breakaway bases. With a 96% reduction in injuries and a 99% reduction in associated health care costs, we felt our conclusion was essentially as close to a no-brainer as one could get.

We submitted the study to *The Journal of the American Medical Association (JAMA)*. Normally, when you submit a study to a prestigious journal such as JAMA, it takes several months to hear back from them. After they decide to review the study, it usually takes another six to nine months before the public sees it. After 2 weeks I got a letter back from the editors. I didn't even open it— I was furious, believing they rejected the study, as there was no way they could have gotten to it so soon. It was that empty feeling all over again. After the anger passed, I did open the letter just to see what reason they gave. Astonished, I couldn't believe it; I had to read it over and over—vindication again. They said that from their preliminary review, they felt that the study was so important and could have such a huge impact on preventing injuries, they planned to fast-track it and publish it right away. The JAMA editors also asked to send our data to the Center for Disease Control and Prevention (CDC) in Atlanta for further statistical analysis. I soon heard from Dr. Rick Waxwiller and Dr. Jeff Sacks, two epidemiologists at the CDC who later became extremely supportive of our efforts at the Institute. At this point, they had a mild interest in the study. They asked me to send them our data. After they received it, they combined it with other data they had collected, and ran an actuarial analysis through their computer system. Based on their analysis of our study, the CDC concluded that if all the fields in the United States were switched from stationary to breakaway bases, it would prevent *approximately 1.7 million injuries a year and save two billion dollars in associated health care costs a year nationally.*

They were amazed by the results and so were we. I asked Rick, "Are you sure you have the decimals right?" "Believe me," he said, "we checked." I was floored. As the most popular team sport in the United States, approximately 40 million people play in recreational, organized softball leagues every year. Americans play an estimated 23 million softball games a year. This does not include pickup games, picnics, youth baseball, teen baseball, or college baseball.

Now, it's interesting. Politicians in Washington and throughout state legislatures across the United States keep trying to cut health care costs by manipulating health care need; i.e., by rationing care and limiting the availability and access to care through HMOs. We demonstrated in just this one study that if you're truly sincere about cutting health care costs, the solution is not to manipulate, but to prevent health care need. It's the single greatest bang for the buck. Here we spent a grand total of $1,000 for this particular study and a federal agency told us we had the potential to save two billion dollars a year in health care costs.

Now granted, we put a tremendous amount of free time in the study. I spent hundreds of hours doing the study with no remuneration. We also had a tremendous number of field supervisors involved and hospital personnel who donated their time to recording these injuries. Even so, with all the phone calls and expenses we ran up, our costs for the study came to roughly $1,000. When you deal with prevention, this cost savings truly is not the exception, but the rule. A very small outlay on prevention can have a significant impact on health care expenditures.

As we concluded the study, my residency was coming to an end. Our work on the rock-hard field of our nation's pastime had energized me and led me to become an enthusiastic advocate of preventative studies. Soon I would be taking my Board exam and making my deal for Allison's health and a lifetime commitment for injury prevention. The Institute for Preventative Sports Medicine became the expression of this commitment.

CHAPTER FOUR

Dream Big

"Dream big and dare to fail."

—Norman Vaughn

I completed my residency July 1, 1989—a day that I thought would never come. The five other orthopedic residents and I agreed to meet at the hospital at 5:00 p.m. and go out on the town to celebrate. We had rented a limo for the occasion. But at 3:00 p.m., I found myself in the operating room with Dr. Kaufer, one of the attending staff in orthopedic surgery. The operation had just begun and I didn't think I would make the celebration. A famous and well-known orthopedic surgeon, Dr. Kaufer later became the chairman of orthopedic surgery at the University of Kentucky. I found him to be a great guy outside of the operating room. In the operating room, he was fair, but demanding, particularly with the junior residents. Nevertheless, he remained cordial and worked well with the residents. We all respected him.

It was getting close to 5:00 p.m. when Dr. Kaufer looked up at the clock on the wall. "Well, Doc," he said, "Your time with us is done. It's time for you to leave."

"Dr. Kaufer," I responded, "We still have at least another hour and a half left before we finish."

"Nope," he said, "I know all you boys have plans. Let's get the third-level residents in here and you go join your fellow graduates."

We shook hands and I scrubbed out of the case. I had ended my servitude and felt great. I was liberated. I ran down to the front door and joined my friends for a triumphant ride around Ann Arbor. We shared a pitcher of beer and celebrated that we didn't have to open a shoe store after all; we'd made it through our five years of training.

I soon accepted a position with Orthopedic Surgery Associates based at St. Joseph's Hospital in Ann Arbor, the largest private practice orthopedic group in the state of Michigan. I became the eighth member of the group. Many of the former attending staff at the university worked at and joined the faculty and staff at St. Joseph's Hospital.

During my earlier interviews, I spoke with the head partner Dr. Bill Heston, who had founded the group 23 years previously. A kind-hearted, mild-mannered guy with a great sense of humor, Bill wanted to know about my interests. I told him I wanted to continue the research that I had started at the university. Allison had not yet become sick and, at this point, I wasn't sure what the nature of that research might be. But by the beginning of August, one month after Allison's illness, when I arrived at Orthopedic Surgery Associates, I knew what I wanted to do. I told Bill that I was adamant about establishing a research institute. I had to focus on prevention and establish an institute; it was nonnegotiable. He wholeheartedly supported the idea, and that conversation launched the Institute for Preventative Sports Medicine.

The Institute at that point, and to this day, is unique. There are thousands of sports medicine organizations around the world and literally hundreds of sports-related research institutes. But no other institute dedicates itself to the issue of prevention. When the Institute opened its doors, several people told me, "Dave, you'll never find the time to develop a prevention institute and you'll never secure the funding to develop a prevention institute." For me, that was like throwing down a gauntlet. I had made the commitment and this resistance only strengthened my resolve.

With Bill's support, we brought the idea to the other members of the Orthopedic Surgery Associates. I told them I wanted to found the Institute, and that I would like it to focus on prevention. Everyone in the group supported the Institute. Throughout the Institute's brief history, the members of Orthopedic Surgery Associates really have been the backbone of the Institute, emotionally, spiritually, and financially. In fact, the Orthopedic Surgery Associates members personally anted up $40,000 of their own money to establish the Institute. No corporate money and no foundation money went into our coffers. The eight members of Orthopedic Surgery Associates footed the bill. So with the money on the table, I went to work.

The first order of business was to create a Board of Directors. We wanted to include not only the members of Orthopedic Surgery Associates, but also others in the medical community with a track record in prevention-related research. The first person I asked and wanted to get involved was Dr. Robert Hensinger, an energetic, outspoken, no-nonsense icon in orthopedic surgery. Dr. Hensinger served as Chief of Pediatric Orthopedic Surgery at the University of Michigan, and later became the President of the American Academy of Orthopedic Surgeons and Chairman of the University of Michigan Orthopedic Surgery department. Among the most well-known and respected orthopedic surgeons in the world, a visionary and a great physician, he has made an enormous difference in my life and many other professional lives. There isn't a day that goes by that I don't hear his voice in my head, telling me something to help keep me out of trouble and, therefore, to help my patients. He truly has been an inspiration to watch in the operating room and in the clinic. Dr. Hensinger also made an enormous difference with the Institute, because he agreed to come on board with the purpose of moving the Institute forward. He opened doors with the American Academy of Orthopedic Surgeons and with other national organizations for recognition of our work.

I next asked Dr. Richard Hawkins. An easygoing, laid-back, happy but extremely driven individual, you may have seen "Hawk" or his partner during the winter Olympic coverage on TV, or on the sidelines administering to downed Denver Broncos. Dr. Hawkins is cofounder of the Stedman-Hawkins Clinic in Vail, Colorado, where they treat many members of the United States Ski Team, and many other athletes around the country, both Olympic and professional. But I knew "Hawk" before he moved to Vail. I had served a reconstructive shoulder fellowship with him at the University of Western Ontario in Canada. An extremely well-known, gifted surgeon, and a gifted individual, I thought it important to get "Hawk" involved. He truly represents, I think, what all of us in medicine should strive for—balance. He balances extremely well the roles of a great husband, a great father, a great physician, and a great researcher. Also a visionary, he always addressed prevention-related issues when he published his shoulder surgery research. Without his help, the Institute would not have progressed as far as it has.

I scored another coup when Derek Mackesy agreed to join the Board. I met Derek during my fellowship with "Hawk" in London, Ontario. A primary care sports medicine physician, Derek did a tremendous amount of work with the Canadian Olympic Hockey program and with many hockey federations around the world. Derek, again, is a visionary and a physician who really touts the role of prevention in his practice.

Derek suggested that we also bring aboard a world-renowned ophthalmologist based in Toronto, Dr. Tom Pashby. A soft-spoken, delightful man, an incredibly gifted physician and again a true visionary, Dr. Pashby literally has prevented thousands of blinding eye injuries. He helped develop face-shields and goalie masks to prevent injuries in hockey. I know of no one who has had more of an impact worldwide on preventing sports injuries than Tom Pashby.

Derek also suggested we contact Dr. Pat Bishop, director of research at the University of Waterloo in Ontario. Pat was integrally involved in the development and use of helmets in hockey, and he has done tremendous research in head and neck impact injuries in sports.

Finally, I spoke to Dr. Rich Salamone about joining our Board. Rich is a very important individual in my life. He and I roomed together at Bucknell during our sophomore, junior, and senior years. Rich is four feet eleven in stature, but about ten feet tall in heart. An Olympic class wrestler, he won a gold medal in the Pan-Am games and was selected to compete as a member of the 1980 Olympic Wrestling Team in the Soviet Union. But because of the boycott of the Olympics, Rich and many other dedicated athletes never had their day in the sun. Rich's accomplishments went far beyond the athletic arena. He completed his doctorate in neuropsychology at Penn State where he met the love of his life, Mary. They moved to Tennessee where he currently practices as a clinical neuropsychologist. Rich has a strong background in medicine; his father was a famous Mayo Clinic trained neurologist. Rich's own background in neuropsychology and sports made him a natural, and we felt very fortunate to have all of these people join the cause.

We next decided that we needed individuals with experience in sports, well-known athletes who, when our research came out, could participate in discussing these issues, could potentially assist us in fund-raising, and help us get our message out to the public. So we formed an Advisory Board.

The first sports celebrity to join the Advisory Board was Walter Payton, the leading rusher in NFL history. I grew up in Chicago, where he was my #1 sports hero. I sent him the material, who better—"dream big, dare to fail." When I sent him information about the Institute, he called back right away to tell me he was glad to come on board and would donate his time. He also said that when I recruited celebrities for the Advisory Board, some of them might ask for money. "You shouldn't have to deal with that," he said. "I'll deal with it. Tell them Walter Payton isn't getting paid and Walter Payton says if anyone asks to get paid, to call him." His comment was indicative of how he was on and off the field. He was one of the greatest athletes ever and gave his all to the sport. But he also gave his all to the community and supported many charitable organizations. His was an example all too rare in professional sports. Professional athletes reap so many rewards, but not all are willing to give back, or else everything they give back has a price on it. Not Walter Payton—he always gave without a thought for himself. In 1999, about a month before he died, we received a box that held a football signed by him. Every year, he sent us something for our annual fund-raiser auction. This time, I knew something was wrong because he usually sent signed items for our auction in January. This time, the box arrived in September. I knew he wasn't going to make it. It was a desperate feeling. He died shortly thereafter, another incredible act of selflessness. He will be greatly missed by all of us at the Institute, though his inspiration remains.

Other notable celebrities who have joined the Advisory Board and helped us include former pro football Hall of Famer John

Unitas; former National League baseball MVP Tommy Davis (Tommy's career was cut short when he slid into a stationary base and broke his leg); former pitching great and past president of the Major League Baseball Players Alumni Association Mud-Cat Grant; Olympic star and television journalist Peggy Fleming; U.S. women's speed skating champion Bonnie Blair; world gymnastics champion many times over and Olympic champion Nadia Comaneci and her husband Olympic gold medalist Bart Conner; and the outstanding major league pitcher well-known for his fight and victory against cancer in his throwing arm, Dave Dravecki.

Many other sports figures joined us as well as leaders and innovators outside the world of sports. Among these who have been the most active and had the biggest impact were Dr. Dave Viano, the principal research scientist at General Motors; Dave Brandon, Chairman of the Board and Chief Executive Office of Domino's Pizza, Inc.; Dave Sowerby, an economist with Loomis Sayles Corporation; Dick Purtan, the Marconi Award winner for the U.S. radio personality of the year; and Jim Dodson, author of the inspirational golf autobiography, *Final Rounds.*

I mentioned the film "Field of Dreams" and the voice I heard when Allison lay sick in the hospital. The film inspired me. So I called the author of the screenplay and the book, Bill Kinsella. He sent a letter accepting a position on the Advisory Board and scribbled a note at the bottom, saying, "Go the distance." I now have the framed letter hanging on my wall in my study at home. So, when things get rough at the Institute or aren't going the way that we would have hoped, I look at the wall and I read that framed letter and keep going the distance.

The Advisory Board has helped us inform many about our studies. We go to them when we want to evaluate an injury pattern and ask them if they actually had seen this pattern when they played their chosen sport. If they say yes, we ask them if they think the interventions that we developed to prevent the injury would work. Often they say, "No, I wouldn't go that route," or "Yes, I would go that route," or "Don't try this because you could never implement it even if it works." This has been a big help and prevented us from going down some dead ends. I could have used them when I suggested "no sliding."

In putting our team together, I recalled Norman Vaughn's words: "Dream big and dare to fail." Norman Vaughn was the chief dog-musher for Admiral Byrd on the Antarctica expedition. Admiral Byrd felt that he never could have accomplished his goal and his exploratory accomplishments without Norman Vaughn's help. For that reason, Byrd named the tallest peak in Antarctica after Norman Vaughn. In some ways I felt like we, too, had embarked on an expedition and like Byrd, I felt that we couldn't succeed without help. Without our Board of Directors, without our Advisory Board, without the media, we never could have accomplished the goals that we set out at the beginning, preventing unnecessary injuries and saving health expenditures.

When he reached 89 years of age, Norman Vaughn went back to Antarctica to climb that peak. By this time, Vaughn had major heart and lung problems and his guides felt that he was going to die on the trip, and would never make it to the peak. He did. When he arrived at the summit, one of the guides asked him, "Mr. Vaughn, how in the world did you do this? You have terrible cardiac difficulties, terrible lung difficulties. You're 89 years of age, you're in a hostile environment in Antarctica. But you've done it." And he said, "It's all about attitude. If you have the right attitude, you can accomplish anything." The guide looked at him and said, "Mr. Vaughn, what do you mean 'attitude?' What attitude?" "It's very, very simple," he said. "Dream big and dare to fail."

And that's what the Institute is all about. It's about dreaming big and daring to fail. I've met a lot of naysayers who felt we could never accomplish our dreams. They saw them as too big. And we have dreamed big. We've dreamed big and we have dared to fail. So far, we've succeeded.

So now we had put our team together and could begin our research. We began where I left off during my residency at the University of Michigan with our breakaway base studies. We had demonstrated that using breakaway bases could prevent 96% of sliding injuries and dramatically cut health care costs. What's more, the study attracted significant media attention, which played a major role in informing the public about prevention. But we still had skeptics who suggested we hadn't done enough testing.

So we decided to approach the recreational leagues in Ann Arbor over the breakaway bases for this study. Actually, we needn't have bothered. This time the players came to us and said they would no longer participate in leagues that used stationary bases. The same players who refused to show up for instructional courses and refused to adopt a no-sliding rule now went to the leagues and *demanded* a change to breakaway bases. They said they would no longer participate on stationary-base fields because they felt that they were hazardous and unsafe. So with this impetus we began our study. We used breakaway bases on all the Ann Arbor fields for 1,400 games. Only two injuries happened during these 1,400 games—two ankle sprains that cost a total of $400 to treat. So the results from our previous study held up—a 98% reduction in injuries and a 99% reduction in associated health care costs.

Despite the results, few recreational leagues adopted break-away bases and we continued to hear criticism about their use. The critics raised four issues:

Breakaway bases will ruin the game. When I asked folks why they felt breakaway bases would ruin the game, they responded, "Breakaway bases will hold up the game because of the time spent setting them back on their moorings after they pop off." So we did a small study and found that when the bases popped off their moorings, they only traveled one or two feet. A player or an umpire could pick them up and set them back in their moorings in roughly 15 seconds. I suggested to folks that if they wanted to hold up a game, play on stationary-base fields, have someone break their ankle or their wrist and wait for the paramedics to show up. Even with the great paramedics we have in our community, it takes at least 15 minutes on average for them to show up. That will definitely hold up a game. Transporting an injured player off the field will take at least another five minutes. So the contention that the bases would ruin the game because they would hold up play was completely off base and erroneous.

Breakaway bases cost more. On one level, they do. At the time of our study, a set of three Rogers bases cost roughly $400 and a set of three stationary bases cost roughly $180. So breakaway bases cost more than twice as much as the stationary bases. How-ever, we found that breakaway bases lasted three times as long. Furthermore, when we replaced the bases on the University of Michigan intramural fields, we only had to replace the base tops, not the stationary part. The base tops only cost $75 per field to replace. More importantly, using breakaway bases prevents injuries, resulting in major health care cost savings. So ultimately, breakaway bases prove far less costly than standard, stationary bases.

Players want an element of danger in the game. If you remove that element of danger, players won't enjoy the game as much. I played a lot of baseball in my day, throughout my youth and teen years and into high school, and I can never remember telling my mom that the reason I loved this sport of baseball was because I might get hurt. I don't know how anyone can argue this on a rational basis.

When you get the pros involved or a lot of colleges involved, we'll consider using them. I believe this, more than any other reason, is why recreational leagues didn't embrace breakaway bases. Baseball is a tradition-bound sport that doesn't welcome change. We would need to overcome a great deal of inertia and resistance if we were to convince leagues to change.

We figured that if we could convince colleges and the professionals to use the bases, this would filter down to the recreational leagues. So we contacted several people in major- and minor-league baseball about our studies. We first spoke to the Detroit Tiger organization and they were not interested in our results. We got the same response from several other professional teams we called around the country.

It looked like we had reached a dead end. I spoke with Dr. Rich Hawkins, our new Board member, about the responses we received from the majors. He spoke with Dr. Peter Fowler, a well-known reconstructive knee surgeon and sports medicine specialist in Canada, and they got things rolling. Pete and Hawk spoke with a friend of theirs, Mr. Paul Beeston, the President of the Toronto Blue Jays and with the Blue Jays soon-to-be general manager, Mr.

Gord Ash. We presented the results of our studies to them and they invited me down to Port St. Lucie, Florida to present our findings to a gathering of several minor-league teams. As a result of the presentation, we convinced 11 minor-league teams to try breakaway bases on their fields.

At about the same time, I presented my findings to officials of the National College Athletic Association meeting in Kansas City. The NCAA didn't act on the findings so I contacted officials for college baseball teams in Michigan and my alma mater, Bucknell. Roger Hall also had a list of college teams that had contacted him about using breakaway bases on their fields. So altogether, 19 minor-league and college baseball teams agreed to participate in a breakaway base study. We ran the study on their fields, using trainers or physicians associated with each school or minor-league baseball team to record injuries.

Paul Beeston and Gord Ash stepped to the plate and initially were the only two individuals within major- or minor-league baseball to embrace the prevention of injury concept. It just didn't make much sense to me. You would think that with the huge salaries owners pay players they would embrace prevention. That's what I said to Jerry Rheinsdorf who owns the Chicago White Sox, and serves as the chairman of the major-league baseball owners' committee. Joe Garagiola put me in touch with Mr. Rheinsdorf after he (Joe Garagiola) did a *Today Show* story on the Institute.

I asked Mr. Rheinsdorf what the impact would be if one of his stars injured himself sliding into a base, and he ended up paying that star six or seven million dollars to sit on the bench for the rest of the year. He shrugged off my question.

I think the owners of major-league baseball did not concern themselves with this issue because essentially they see their players as commodities, just as they might see any other commodity.

They could depreciate the value lost to injury and have their accountants write it off, so it wasn't a big deal to them.

I also contacted the major-league baseball players' association and they seemed completely indifferent to addressing sliding injuries. I found it odd that they appeared disinterested in attempting to lengthen the careers of the players that they represented. Nevertheless with the help of Paul Beiston and Gord Ash and with the support of the Toronto Blue Jays organization, we ended up performing a breakaway bases study with professional and other high performance players. At the conclusion of the first year of the study, the results supported the use of breakaway bases. We received positive feedback from all the players and managerial staffs. Nevertheless, I received a call from Chuck Murphy, head of the minor-league baseball organization, saying that they wanted to end the study. I asked him why, since the results had been so positive. He said that major-league baseball didn't want the study to continue. Apparently, the stationary-base manufacturers, who had a long-standing relationship with major-league baseball, had convinced major-league baseball officials that it wouldn't be a good idea to continue the study. Major-league baseball then put the squeeze on minor-league baseball.

I spoke to Tommy Davis, Mud Cat Grant, and other former major-league players on our Advisory Board. We made some calls to major-league executives, including National League President Bill White and suggested that if they ended the study and brought it to a premature conclusion, the media would be alerted and they would have to answer to the public.

The next day, I received another phone call from Chuck Murphy. He said that he had heard from major-league baseball and we had been given the green light to complete the second year of the study. So we completed the study, and found that even the minor-league and college players, with much greater conditioning and training and playing on much better-kept fields, saw an 80% reduction in injuries when using breakaway bases. Individuals such as Bill Murray, Director of Baseball Operations for major league baseball, and Stephen Greenberg, Deputy Commissioner, had suggested that professionals and high-level college athletes would not benefit from the use of breakaway bases because they are so good at the technique of sliding. But we found that breakaway bases could prevent 80% of these players' injuries.

So we concluded that no matter what the level of play—youth, teen, adult, college, recreation, professional—players benefited from using breakaway bases. Despite these findings, breakaway bases received no further consideration from the pros and, although we've made some inroads, they still haven't been widely adopted in recreational leagues. Why haven't they been more widely adopted? I believe we need to look at the role of some sporting goods manufacturers for an answer to this question.

CHAPTER FIVE

The Field of Schemes

"Always do right. This will gratify some and astonish the others."

—MARK TWAIN

The inventor of the Lego® type breakaway base is Roger Hall, a former college baseball coach from Elizabethtown, Pennsylvania. A tall, thin wiry man, Roger looks a little like Thomas Edison, and may be his reincarnation. A brilliant inventor in his own right, Roger is an inveterate tinkerer and an all-around visionary of the possibilities. He genuinely loves baseball and sincerely wants to see the game become safer and more fun for kids and young adults. He invented the breakaway base after a friend of his broke a thighbone after sliding into a stationary base 15 years prior to our research. His friend suffered complications from the injury and subsequently died from a blood clot that migrated to his lungs. Roger was devastated by his friend's death and didn't want to see anyone else suffer the injuries and pain his friend had sustained. So he decided to find a way to prevent sliding injuries. For the next eight years, he spent all his spare time working in his garage at home. He experimented with many different solutions before finally coming upon the idea of constructing a base made of a rubber mat with rubber thumbs on the top over which the break-away portion would snap into place. He spent many months perfecting and testing his breakaway base. Finally, Roger took his invention to university medical schools and sporting goods communities, up and down the East Coast. Unfortunately, he found very little support for the breakaway base, primarily because he didn't have any financial backers. He was an inventor, not a marketer nor a financier, and he didn't have the resources to promote his product. Because he had no money to support research, no university would agree to conduct a study on the effectiveness of the bases. They wanted money to do the research and no one felt sports injury prevention was important. It's sad, but true, that few universities actually conduct independent research. All too often, they will only test products for manufacturers who agree to fund the research or when government money is available. This financial relationship seriously undermines the credibility of such research and can betray the public interest. The point is that for Roger this became a vicious cycle; he couldn't afford to fund research, and because he didn't have the research to back up his claims, no one took his product seriously.

At this point, Roger's story begins to resemble that of Preston Tucker, the engineer who in 1948 built the car of the future, the Tucker Torpedo, only to have his factory shut down by the big auto manufacturers. Like Tucker, Roger needed financing and the only assistance he could obtain was to strike a deal with the devil, in this case, the Hollywood Base Company. They bought the marketing and distribution rights to the base and then basically spent no money on promoting or distributing it. Instead, they let the Rogers Break-Away Base languish on their shelves for several years. The company had no interest in promoting a better product that might compete with their own stationary base.

Roger did have advocates within the company, namely Rick Porter, the product supervisor who serviced his account. Rick is the individual I first spoke to when I called the Hollywood Base Company to inquire about the Rogers Break-Away Base. Rick sincerely believed in the product and tried to promote it. Unfortunately, without the support of the Hollywood Base executives, Rick got nowhere. It wasn't very long after my initial phone call to his office that Rick was fired, and Roger's relationship with the Hollywood Base Company began to sour.

At any rate, this is when we first stepped into the picture. As I mentioned, when I first spoke with Rick, he told me that they had attempted to convince many universities to test the breakaway base, but none would step to the plate. Fortuitously, they had independently come to the conclusion that improperly sliding into bases could cause devastating injuries. In fact, as our research later demonstrated, almost two million injuries occurred annually from improperly sliding into bases at a cost to the American taxpayer of $2 billion annually in health care costs. The Institute had a common interest with Roger and Rick in our desire to find a method to prevent or at least significantly reduce these injuries.

Because I didn't want to taint our study, I didn't speak with or meet Roger before it was published. After the *Journal of the American Medical Association* accepted the study, I called Roger, a call of vindication, to let him know of our findings, and to tell him that the study would be published. There was a light at the end of the tunnel. From the moment I first spoke with Roger, I found him to be enthusiastic, energetic, full of ideas, and one of the most honest, sincere individuals I have ever met. Articulate and very soft-spoken, he knew the nuances of softball injuries. He talked on and on about the welfare of people playing games. The issue of money never came into our conversation. For many in the sports world, money would have been mentioned in the first two sentences. Unfortunately, as I mentioned, his brilliance at developing sports equipment didn't carry over into his aptitude for financing or marketing his ideas. The marketing and distributing agreement with the Hollywood Base Company had provided him with some hope of developing the resources he needed to succeed. Unfortunately, by the time our study was published, Roger's relationship with the Hollywood Base Company had gone from bad to worse. The company tried to convince him to hand over the patent to them; in return, they would give him a royalty fee. Roger refused and the company began to actively oppose his efforts to market his product. The agreement between Roger and Hollywood Base Company had run out and Roger had the rights back. That was when I discovered how a few sporting goods manufacturers (not just the Hollywood Base Company) had forsaken the field of dreams for the field of schemes. They had lost their way and no longer saw a purpose in promoting fun and safety in sports. Instead, their major concern became making a buck, and they would do anything, including undercutting efforts to develop new equipment that could prevent sports injuries.

Following publication of the study, requests for breakaway bases inundated Roger. But without the production capabilities or distribution channels of a large manufacturer like the Hollywood Base Company, Roger couldn't meet the demand. He tried to obtain financing from several banks, only to be told they couldn't help. I wouldn't be surprised to discover that executives at the Hollywood Base Company and several other stationary base companies had asked their friends in the banking industry to deny Roger financing for producing his product. After approaching dozens of banks without success, Roger finally stumbled upon some venture capitalists, who agreed to fund the first several shipments of his product. They convinced Roger that the product would lose money unless they went offshore to produce it and soon struck a deal with a production plant in Taiwan. It looked like they were in business. But in August 1989, shortly after production began, Roger received a fax from the production plant stating that they were having difficulty producing the bases because of problems with the tooling. Roger asked for more information and was told that a Mr. Ron Bartoli of Hollywood Base Company had called the tooling company and asked them to stop making the molds. Incredible.

So, first several stationary base companies potentially tried to undermine the financing. When that failed, they attempted to block production of the breakaway base. Fortunately, Roger eventually succeeded in obtaining the tooling, and the plant resumed production of the breakaway bases. However, production and distribution continue to be modest to this date and have never reached the levels they might have, with the support of a major manufacturer. In the intervening years, the Hollywood Base Company continued to work against the interests of the public by undermining distribution of the breakaway base and misrepresenting the product to leagues and officials. They did everything they could to prevent the use of breakaway bases solely because they didn't have a financial interest in the product. During trade shows and on business calls, they would tell people that breakaway bases were inferior, that our studies were wrong, and that the product shouldn't be used. I firmly believe that one of the reasons major league baseball refused to adopt breakaway bases had to do with its ties either through licensing agreements and/or fees to the Hollywood Base Company and other stationary base manufacturers.

It wasn't just the stationary base manufacturers that schemed to make more money at the expense of the public. As I mentioned earlier, the Rogers Break-Away base is a Lego® type base that snaps on over rubber thumbs or grommets. In our initial research, we investigated several types of breakaway bases, including magnetic breakaway bases and Velcro breakaway bases. However, we decided against using these products in our study because we found that if dirt or water lodged in between them, they became unstable and popped off with very little force. They became so unstable, in fact, that the bases actually led to, rather than prevented injury.

About six months after our study was published in the *Journal of the American Medical Association*, I began to receive phone calls from throughout the United States and Canada about one of these products, the magnetic breakaway base. Inevitably, the conversation began, "We used that magnetic breakaway base that you said would be effective, but in fact, people have been injured with these bases." I usually responded, "We never used the magnetic bases in our studies. What makes you think we did" And they would reply, "Your name appears in these magnetic base advertisements. You're quoted in these ads as saying that you tested these bases in your study, and that they will prevent injuries from occurring." I was horrified, shocked, and livid beyond anything I had ever felt. I had to get to the bottom of this.

Following one of these conversations, I asked the caller to send me a copy of the advertisement. The ad, indeed, liberally quoted me, as well as Jeff Sacks from the Center for Disease Control. Furthermore, it said that the Institute's research supported use of the magnetic release base for reducing sliding injuries.

My heart sank. After all of the work we had done to prevent injuries, we found our efforts undercut by fraudulent advertising. We had not used the magnetic release base in our study because we knew from reports and from examining them that they were ineffective and would not reduce injuries. The ad referred to the manufacturer of the magnetic bases, Megg-Nets, USA, and listed the address and phone number of their office in Roseville, Minnesota. I called the number and asked to speak with their spokesperson, Mr. Ron Foyt. He took my call, but told me that he had nothing to do with the advertising—that the parent company in Canada had paid for the ad. He indicated that if I had a beef, I should speak with them. He then referred me to the corporate headquarters in Ayr, Ontario, Canada, and suggested I speak to either Mr. Riley or Mr. Meggs.

I called Riley-Meggs Industries in Ayr, Ontario, Canada and was connected to Mr. Riley. I will remember that conversation to my dying day. It was one of the worst examples of corporate arrogance I've ever encountered.

I expressed my concerns to Mr. Riley he said, "Look, buddy. You should be grateful for the free advertising. We sent out approximately 250,000 of these ads with your name on it and that's a great advertisement for you. And we didn't charge you anything. Furthermore, you don't have the time or the effort or the money to take us to court and sue us."

I bellowed at him, "That's fraud, we didn't study your product and it doesn't work!!"—at which point I slammed the phone down. Another resident who was in the room, Matt Beuche, looked at me and asked "Was he in Canada?" "Yes", I replied. "I don't think he needed a phone to hear you."

Well, as far as the first point, I didn't see it as free advertising, I saw it as fraudulent advertising that duped the public into using a truly defective and injurious product. Furthermore, the ad damaged our reputation by making false claims that we used their product in our study. As for Mr. Riley's second point, unfortunately for him, my wife Libby is a practicing attorney in the state of Michigan and we took his company to court.

Before we took this step, I spoke to Ed Goldman, one of the foremost attorneys for the University of Michigan. I had worked with him before and found him to be a very nice man, soft-spoken, mild-mannered, conscientious, and one who thinks before he speaks, a trait I am far from mastering. I asked if the university would join us in our suit against Riley-Meggs. He said that they did not want to participate in the lawsuit because they just didn't have the time or the finances to do so. I next contacted the Center for Disease Control (the Riley-Meggs fraudulent advertising mentioned them as well). They also told me that they didn't have the financial backing or the time to put into such a lawsuit. So "little ole" Dave Janda, physician and independent researcher, ended up pursuing the case, with Libby, while a state university and the federal government looked the other way.

This occasion was one of many when I was told, "No, you can't do that," or "No, you shouldn't do that." And on this, as on the other occasions, I went ahead because I felt an obligation to the public and a commitment to the prevention of unnecessary injuries. Furthermore, I believed I had to fulfill my obligation to that higher power that had started me on this quest. I believed that by not following through and pursuing this suit, I would be compromising myself and undercutting the Institute and our purpose.

The Institute, therefore, pursued the case on its own and took it to state court. After the filing, we appeared in court on several occasions, and heard continuance after continuance. After a year, the case was bounced up into federal court at Riley-Meggs' insistence. We were concerned that Riley-Meggs' foot-dragging might be an attempt to manipulate its accounts and shuffle the money around. Companies sometimes do this in legal cases so that it appears very few funds are available to pay a settlement. But we pressed on until the case finally made it to a federal court two years later.

On May 1, 1991, we appeared in front of Judge Paul J. Gadola. My wife, Libby, and her firm, Brooks and Kushman of Southfield, Michigan, represented me. Libby, and one of her partners, Mark Cantor, served as my attorneys on that fateful day. Before the trial, we had several pretrial conferences. This was during the height of the very popular TV show, "LA Law." Mark and Libby told me that this trial would be nothing like "LA Law" or anything else on television. They told me I should just answer their questions and not say anything extemporaneously to the judge. "Don't start telling a story to the judge," Libby told me. "Just answer our questions."

The trial began. After about 15 minutes, I sensed that the judge was leaning our way. So I resolved to have my say when I took the stand. Finally, Mark Cantor called me as a witness. Libby sat at the plaintiff's table while Mark began to question me. I didn't answer his question, but rather turned to the judge and said, "Let me tell you what all this is about." I was so relieved to finally have this at trial—I knew we could win if I could just tell my story and I couldn't stop. I told him the whole story about why we did our study, how we did the study, our findings, the study's impact on the public and the cost savings to the public. I then noted that by linking our study to a fraudulent piece of advertising for a defective product, Riley-Meggs had misled the public and betrayed its trust. I conversed with the judge for a good half-hour.

At one point the judge looked up at Mark and said, "You can sit down." I looked over to the table. Libby had her head in her hands.

When I was finished, the judge turned to Ron Foyt, who was representing himself and the Riley-Meggs subsidiary in the United States, and asked him several pertinent questions. "Do you have any disagreements with the facts as Dr. Janda presented them?" Mr. Foyt said "No." "Do you have any evidence that contradicts what Dr. Janda just told me?" Mr. Foyt again said "no." Needless to say, he could not defend himself because the facts rested on our side, and the fraud with him and his company.

The judge dismissed court. Several weeks later, he rendered a decision in our favor. He ruled that Riley-Meggs pay our attorneys' legal fees. Furthermore, he issued an injunction against Mr. Foyt and Riley-Meggs Industries ordering them to stop using the Institute's name, my name, and our research in their ads, and ordered them to pay us a significant sum of moneys.

I was thoroughly ecstatic because we had won a major victory for prevention, plus, the Institute had won some money to support its efforts. What happened next seriously undermined my faith in the legal system. Essentially, we had a big decision go our way. The court had ruled in our favor. Ron Foyt and the Riley-Meggs subsidiary in the U.S. claimed bankruptcy and shifted their operations to Canada.

In essence, Riley-Meggs thumbed their noses at us and essentially told Harry Drummond, our attorney in Canada, "OK, Yankee. You won down south, but you'll never win up here in Canada. We're not going to pay you a penny." And, in fact, they never did. Furthermore, they continued to allude to our research in their advertisement, even with a federal injunction against them.

Libby and I spent our own money to pay legal fees in Canada, which dragged on for another four years. We endured the trial court in Canada, the appellate court, and then our equivalent of the state supreme court with the associated appeals. We have won on every level in the Canadian court system. We found this a truly frustrating experience, because unlike in the United States courts, if you lose at one level in the Canadian courts, you don't have to prove a violation of precedent or procedure to appeal. You can just say, "We lost, so we appeal." Unfortunately, Riley-Meggs Industries is a multimillion dollar corporation, and the Institute and the Janda family are very short-ball hitters financially. Riley-Meggs felt, and may ultimately prove right, that the longer they could string the case out and ante up the legal fees, the better chance they have of winning. And, the ultimate loser, besides the Institute, is the public, because they continue to be misled by this company's fraudulent advertising.

In early 2000 we got hit with a double whammy, our legal counsel died, and after investigating the financial state of Riley-Meggs Industries, we found out our suspicions appeared to have become reality—after years of court battles, no money was left for our judgment—so we cut our losses and settled. Justice was not done! Yet, in April of 2003 it came to my attention that Riley launched a website again linking my name, The Institute and our studies to his product—the fraud and deception of the public continues!

We can do the best research in the world, but if it is misrepresented to the public, we won't prevent injuries, and we won't diminish health care costs. Unscrupulous, deceitful individuals will continue to make money, hand over fist, while others continue to be injured.

Individuals such as Riley and Riley-Meggs Industries give all of corporate North America a bad name. With them, money truly comes first, and people second. "Whatever it takes to get ahead" is their creed. Even when a federal court has decided against them, they continued to deceive the public. And players continue to sustain unnecessary injuries. Unfortunately, our experience with the sporting goods industry suggests that there are many players on this field of schemes. Certainly, there are many good people in the industry. Unfortunately, the bad ones seem to have the upper hand at the moment.

Hollywood Base Company came back into the picture on April 23, 1993, when they sent a letter under the name of a Mr. Larry Brushett to the American Academy of Orthopedic Surgeons and other organizations. These organizations included athletic equipment trade journals, softball and baseball organizations, and other athletic organizations throughout the United States. The letter stated that the Hollywood Base Company had recently conducted a study on a modified type of stationary base called the "impact base." This base didn't break away upon impact. Instead it compressed more than a standard base, i.e., it squished more.

According to the letter, the study found that their base was actually a "safer" base than the Roger Hall base for softball and baseball. Furthermore, the letter significantly misrepresented and belittled our previous studies and suggested that our studies were more limited than theirs. Upon examination, it became clear that their study lacked scientific merit, was poorly thought out, poorly implemented, and poorly analyzed. Furthermore, it included no credible statistical analysis and, to top it off, was paid for by the Hollywood Base Company. At this point, Libby and her firm came to the rescue once again. They fired off several letters and shut their misrepresentation down.

Subsequently, we did an updated study in our lab that looked at all types of breakaway bases and modified stationary bases, including the impact base. The biomechanical data that we generated contradicted their findings. The impact bases were still fixed and relatively immovable and the amount of compression that took place when a player slid into them was not sufficient to reduce injury.

Unfortunately, we were the victims of the not uncommon practice in which companies misrepresent or ignore independent peer-reviewed research and fund bogus studies to push their own product. It's a problem that we face in sports medicine and in medicine generally. How can we trust studies funded by manufacturers who have a vested interest in the product? Whether it's a base manufacturer or a pharmaceutical company, the outcome is a foregone conclusion and such "research" is seriously detrimental to the public interest. In the year 2000, pharmaceutical companies have embraced independent research, unlike the sporting goods industry. And, truly, one has to question the science involved when marketing replaces research. For this reason, the Institute has never taken nor will it ever take a penny from a sporting goods manufacturer for any of its research. We believe this would undermine the independent nature of our research. Furthermore, we believe this independent stance should become the norm in medicine rather than the exception.

The letter from the Hollywood Base Company did not dupe the American Academy of Orthopedic Surgeons and they continue to support our research endeavors. It appears some organizations had been duped, however, and bought in to the argument that they could stay with a Hollywood Base Company product and still prevent injuries. Unfortunately, as Henry David Thoreau said, "It takes two to speak the truth—one to speak, and another to hear." And unfortunately, the ultimate losers, again, are the public, who continue to sustain needless injuries.

The Hollywood Base Company and Riley-Meggs provided several instances of business ethics at its worst. Unfortunately, these were only the first of several such encounters we experienced in our dealings with unscrupulous sporting goods manufacturers. As our research proceeded in other directions, we discovered many new players on the field of schemes.

CHAPTER SIX

A Grunt Goes to Washington

"After lots of people who go into politics have been in it for a while, they find that, to stay in politics, they have to make all sorts of compromise to satisfy their supporters, and that it becomes awfully important for them to keep their jobs because they have nowhere else to go."

—ADLAI STEVENSON

"Injury is probably the most under-recognized major public health problem facing the nation today, and the study of injury represents unparalleled opportunities for reducing morbidity and mortality, and for realizing significant savings in both financial and human terms, all in return for a relatively modest investment."

—NATIONAL ACADEMY OF SCIENCE,
INJURY CONTROL, 1988

The above statement, now a decade and a half old, is as true today as it was then. Unfortunately, little has occurred in the way of injury prevention since then, primarily because of the complete indifference of medical researchers, politicians, and insurance executives. Injuries from all causes kill more than 142,000 Americans per year and result in more than 62 million individuals requiring medical attention annually. The single greatest killer of individuals ages one to forty-four, cost the nation over 150 billion dollars a year. Many of these are sports related. In 1999, over 1 million baby boomers, ages 35 to 54, were injured in sports just in the United States and this figure has increased by 33% over the past seven years. In Canada the most common cause of injury in the 15 to 24 year age group are sports injuries.

The United States Consumer Products Safety Commission (CPSC) reports that athletes receive medical treatment for five million sports injuries annually. Youth sports injuries, in particular, are common. Nearly 3% of elementary students participating in sports sustain an injury every year; while 7% of junior high students, and 11% of high school students sustain an injury annually. About 20% of these injuries require hospitalization. The CPSC figures suggest that four million school age student athletes annually will receive emergency room treatment for a sports-related injury treated and another eight million will report sports injuries to physician offices.

Large numbers of sports injuries occur among adults as well. Department of Defense documents list sports injuries as the leading cause for days missed in the United States military. They also listed sports injuries as the leading cause for air evacuations during the Persian Gulf War. And this isn't just a national phenomenon. A recent study by the New South Wales government in Sydney, Australia revealed that, over a two-year time frame, 54% of students participating in sports in New South Wales's high schools sustained a sports-related injury. With increasing worldwide participation in sports, injuries have become an epidemic of global proportions.

Those of us on the front line of health care delivery feel frustrated and perplexed by the apparent inability of government, business, and medical research facilities to focus on the issue of injury and injury prevention. For several years, I attempted, without much success, to involve government officials and business leaders in injury prevention. After countless calls to state legislators, insurance executives, and business leaders and little to no response, I had just about given up hope. So I was dumbfounded when one day, just after the November 1988 election of George Bush, a secretary in my clinic held up the phone and told me that someone from the White House wanted to speak with me.

I picked up the phone convinced that one of my friends was playing a practical joke; they knew that I had recently written an article in one of the Washington papers about sports injuries prevention and its effect on curtailing health care expenditures. The very pleasant woman on the phone informed me that President-elect Bush had an active interest in sports and prevention of injuries because of his baseball experience; he served as the captain of the Yale baseball team. In addition, the woman informed me that then-President Reagan had for a number of years maintained an avid interest in sports, going back to his days as a sports broadcaster. She further informed me that President-elect Bush and President Reagan had read my article in one of the Washington periodicals and were interested in my involvement in health care cost containment.

"You've done a wonderful job," I told her. "Just tell me who put you up to this practical joke and I'll be happy to call back and let him know you did a great job. You were very convincing, and you really had me going." She informed me that this was not a joke and she was calling from the White House. "If this truly is someone from the White House, give me your phone number and I'll call you back," I said, knowing full well that any phone number she gave me certainly would not ring at the White House. She gave me a number. I hung up the phone and redialed. The White House switchboard operator answered and connected me to the woman who had placed the call. I was not only incredulous, but extremely embarrassed. I apologized profusely, my mind was reeling with what they wanted, would they want me to go to Washington? Could I make a difference?

The woman told me that the congressman in our district, Carl Purcell, and his administrative assistant, Bill McBride, would call me about delivering our message of injury prevention and health care cost containment before a health care related congressional committee.

Very soon thereafter, just as promised, Bill McBride, the administrative assistant to Congressman Purcell, called me. We talked and agreed that I would testify with Congressman Purcell before the House Appropriations Subcommittee on Labor, Education, Health and Human Services. Bill McBride suggested that while I visited Washington, I should discuss the issues with as many individuals as possible, including Lee Atwater, then chairman of the Republican National Committee, and other individuals in the Republican National Committee.

As I saw it, this was it, a modern day *Mr. Smith Goes to Washington,* or in this case, a Grunt Goes to Washington and it wasn't a movie. I was pumped up and flying high. I was ready to hit Washington running hard and fast.

I arrived $1\frac{1}{2}$ hours early at Detroit Metropolitan Airport on a very cool spring morning; I boarded a plane and flew to National Airport in Washington, DC, where I took a cab to Congressman Purcell's office. It was a small, sparsely furnished office with pictures on the wall of Congressman Purcell meeting various celebrities and political figures. Bill McBride introduced me to the congressman and I sat down. They were both friendly, soft-spoken, quiet people. Both expressed (and continue to express) a sincere interest in injury prevention and health care cost containment. You would think interest in such issues would be the rule in Washington, yet over the years, I have found it to be the exception. We spoke for a while and they briefed me on what would happen in the testimony before the committee. Then Bill walked me over to the committee hearing room.

The room was a huge auditorium with an elaborate paneled bench. There were multiple committeemen and their staffs positioned in this stately place of authority.

Before I testified, the actress Mary Tyler Moore appeared before the committee. She spoke about the need for funding the Juvenile Diabetes Foundation. A tireless spokesperson and fundraiser on behalf of the Juvenile Diabetes Foundation, Ms. Moore has helped tens of thousands of individuals battle one of the most difficult diseases that can afflict an individual. I was very interested in and impressed with her testimony. The members of Congress also listened intently. Unfortunately, as I was soon to find out, such is not the case with less high profile individuals testifying before Congress.

Ms. Moore finished and another attestant stood up to testify. He failed to capture anywhere near the same level of interest among the members of the committee. In fact, throughout his entire testimony, the congressmen continued to talk among themselves and largely ignored him. I turned to one of Congressman Purcell's aides and asked, "Why aren't they paying attention to this fellow's testimony?"

This was standard fare, the aide said. When someone submits a written statement, the members of Congress don't necessarily pay attention to the spoken testimony, and when time runs out, they kindly thank the attestant and move on to the next person's testimony. I told the aide I wouldn't let this happen when I testified. If Congress listened to Mary Tyler Moore and gave her their attention, they should listen to an ordinary person like me. If I took the time and effort and expense to leave the health care battlefield and come speak to the generals, then the generals should listen. The aide gave me a whimsical look that seemed to say, "Best of luck buddy! It ain't going to happen!"

The fellow testifying before me finished and, just as the aide predicted, the committee summarily dismissed him, thanked him and called me to testify almost in the same breath. Mr. Natcher, a congressman from Kentucky and the chairman of the committee, motioned me forward. An absolute fixture and significant power broker in the House of Representatives, he appeared cordial and pleasant and not at all intimidating as I sat down to testify. I began to speak. About 45 seconds into my testimony, I noticed that several of Congressman Natcher's aides approached him and began a conversation. I continued and pretty soon a couple of other congressmen on the committee started talking among themselves. I figured we could either continue with this charade or I could make them remember Dave Janda and his testimony.

So I stopped, swallowed hard and said, with my voice getting stronger and more forceful as I went on, "Congressman Natcher, do you have a question for me? It's obvious that you must, because you're talking to your aides. I prefer that you ask me the question rather than your aides so that we can come to a quicker answer."

This comment appeared to take him off guard, as he paused, looking directly at me. He looked down at me and said in a Southern drawl, "Well sir, no, I don't have a question for you. I was just talking to some of my aides about another important matter."

I responded with full confidence, feeling I had his attention, thinking maybe this little guy was full of fire and brimstone and not to be put down, "That's fine Mr. Chairman, but if you're done now, what I'll do is start over. I'd hate for you to miss any of my testimony, because it contains significant information which you haven't heard before and I want you to be aware of it."

He looked at me and I think he actually appreciated the candor. "Well, why don't you start all over again?" he said. So I did. I continued with my testimony. I outlined the magnitude of the injury problem, the economic consequences, and the positive effects of injury prevention research, including major reductions in health care costs. My testimony won the full attention of every congressman on that committee and I felt a little like Mary Tyler Moore that day, or at least like Dick Van Dyke.

At the conclusion of my testimony, Congressman Natcher struck his gavel with an echo across the room, dismissing the other congressmen. He then motioned me closer. "You know," he said. "Every individual that testifies before our committee asks for money; you didn't. How much do you want?" I think my answer took him back even more than my previous interruption.

"Congressman Natcher," I said. "I don't want any money."

"You don't want any money?" he said, looking puzzled.

"None of us want any money from you or your committee or from Washington DC for that matter. What the government can do is shine light on this issue, publicize it and better inform the public." I went on to say that if the public were informed on the issues of injury and injury prevention, the funding would automatically occur. "All we need is public awareness, not funds," I told him. "The funds should come from private citizens and corporations, not from the taxpayer." Congressman Natcher just shook his head. How would Congress publicize it? He seemed genuinely surprised that someone appeared before Congress and didn't ask for money.

Congressman Purcell then came over and congratulated me on my testimony. He patted me on the back and shook my hand

and was kind and gracious. Meanwhile, Bill McBride had just returned to the room. He told me that he had heard through the grapevine about my "antics" in front of the Committee. He laughed and spoke with glee about how "I had the stones" to interrupt Congressman Natcher and ask to repeat my testimony from the beginning. He laughed again when he heard that Congressman Natcher had asked me about funding, and that I told him I didn't want any money. Bill got the biggest kick from someone being brutally honest with all the congressmen. I found the experience extremely enlightening.

Congressman Purcell's office had also arranged for me to visit the Republican National Committee and speak with members about the issues of health care cost containment and injury prevention. Immediately after my testimony, I walked over to the Republican National Committee headquarters. There I met with the chief-of-staff to the chairman of the Republican National Committee, Bill Crump from Mississippi, a staunch supporter of health care cost containment and injury prevention. Very few people in Washington seem interested in our very commonsense approach to health care cost containment. In fact, I can name them on one hand. One of these supporters, a fellow wandering through the Republican National Committee office playing the guitar, was Lee Atwater the chairman of the Republican Party. Every description I had ever heard about Lee Atwater portrayed him as incredibly intense, and at times, at least according to the media, vicious. This guy appeared to be having the time of his life while performing his poor rendition of a country western singer in search of a band, as well as a melody.

He introduced himself. "I understand you have some pretty good ideas about cutting health care costs and helping people," he said.

I responded, "Well yes sir, I think I do."

"Let's sit down and talk," he said. "We'll get Bill Crump involved and see what we can do to get this information to the folks who can make a difference." Now I had shifted from an excitement of anticipation into an excitement of results. I felt he was a doer; he got things done, and fast.

I found this encounter interesting because Mr. Atwater (at least in my eyes, and of course I'm very biased on this issue) represented the Republican Party's vision and in particular George Bush's vision. I came to learn this was true in future meetings in Washington with individuals from his office and people in the White House. Sadly, about a year and a half after we met, he sustained a seizure while giving a speech and was diagnosed with brain cancer. He was in his early forties. The day that I heard the report of his brain cancer, I told Libby that it was the beginning of the end for the Bush presidency. I knew from my experience with Lee Atwater that he was the conduit between the president and the American public. When George Bush lost his conduit, George Bush lost his vision and his connection with the American public. The best way to describe Lee Atwater is that he served as a political internet, an information highway, transferring information into and out of the White House. I believe Lee Atwater's illness and his subsequent death ultimately proved responsible for George Bush losing the presidency in 1992.

My day in Washington passed like a whirlwind—the briefing with Congressman Purcell, testifying before the congressional committee, meeting with members of the Republican National Committee, then back for a late lunch with Bill McBride and Congressman Purcell, followed by introductions to several members of the House and Senate.

These introductions caused me to reflect back to my senior year in high school when I last had the opportunity to meet several congressmen and senators in Washington. I began working on a science project in seventh and eighth grade which won awards at the state level. I continued developing it through my four years in high school. The project dealt with civil engineering and metallurgy, specifically measuring corrosion and weathering effects in metals. Finally, I entered the project in the National Westinghouse Science Talent Search Competition. That year, over 14,000 entered the Westinghouse Science Talent Search. They selected 40 as winners and invited them to Washington. Not long after I submitted my entry, I received a phone call from the folks in the Science Talent Search. They told me they had selected me as one of the Science Talent Search winners and invited me to Washington. I grew up in the suburbs of Chicago, and my representative at the time was Ed Derwinski, who later became the head of the Veterans Administration for President Bush. While I was in Washington, his extremely gracious secretary took me around and introduced me to Adlai Stevenson, Charles Percy, Scoop Jackson, Edmund Muskie, and Hubert Humphrey.

But the individual that I remembered the most was Ted Kennedy. As I mentioned, I grew up in the southwest suburbs of Chicago, a Republican stronghold. My grandparents and my parents were Republicans. They told me that not only don't you vote for Democrats, but my gosh, if you do go to Washington and you see any Kennedy, particularly Ted Kennedy, run the other way. When I met Senator Kennedy in the hallway, he smiled and shook my hand and asked me about my project, unlike the other senators. He asked me how I won the award and what it was all about. His kindness bewildered me because this guy seemed nice; I thought he was supposed to be a bad guy. I mean a real nasty guy. At least that's what I had been taught. As he put his arm over my shoulders and we walked down one of the corridors of the capitol, I had a vision of my Republican grandparents spinning in their graves.

When I finished explaining my project to him, he looked at me and he said, "I wish you all the best of luck. And boy, I'll tell you, we need more folks like you coming here and talking to us about science and issues that could help people."

I immediately said to him, "Senator, this has been very nice of you to take the time and effort to talk to a high school kid, but I'm not sure I understand."

He looked at me, maybe surprised by my reply and a forebear of my frankness with politicians, and said, "What don't you understand?"

"Well, sir," I responded. "I'm from a very Republican family and I'm not supposed to like you. You really seem to be a good guy though."

He smiled and said, "Let's just keep that between the two of us. You don't have to tell your parents that they were wrong!" I found him, at least on that day, to be very gracious and extremely nice.

But my latest foray into the halls of Congress left me feeling rather less impressed and significantly more frustrated, especially with one senator telling me, "Physicians have no place in trying to influence health care reform." My experience reminded me of a few words of wisdom from Will Rogers: "Politics is the best show in America. I love animals and I love politicians and I love to watch both of them play, either back home in their native state or after they have been captured and sent to the zoo or to Washington."

Following my testimony, Congress did little to increase public awareness of prevention and health care costs. At first I thought my testimony had no impact, but it did have some. Several months later, Congress recommended that all military and federal penitentiary institutions in the country switch their playing fields from stationary to breakaway bases. Based on my testimony, United States military bases throughout the world switched over to breakaway bases. The federal penitentiary system also switched its playing fields over to breakaway bases. At that point, the vast majority of baseball and softball players in the United States weren't playing on fields with breakaway bases, but Charles Manson was playing softball on safer fields. I have the privilege of knowing that I have probably prevented ankle sprains and fractures among the mass murderers of our country. Meanwhile, the vast majority of our law-abiding public received little benefit from my testimony—at least in the short term.

The other major impact of my testimony in Congress was that over time I began to receive government appointments related to sports injury prevention. My views on health care cost containment through prevention also provided me with the opportunity to meet members of the Domestic Policy Council in the White House as well as the Economic Policy Council of the White House. (These bodies develop policy and economic initiatives for the president to present to the public and Congress.)

I also developed some close allies on the beltway who later became friends. John Schall, in particular became a good friend. One of the leaders of the Domestic Policy Council, John was later chief-of-staff to Secretary of Labor Lynn Martin.

John believes that individuals on the front line in health care should have an active role within government and in developing government health care policy. One might expect the view that those who serve in the front lines should be involved in making policy would be a common belief in Washington. Unfortunately, such is not the case. I've spoken to several government officials and policy makers within different administrations and I must say that John's philosophy differs greatly from the vast majority. Most believe that only government officials within the beltway know what needs to happen; folks beyond the beltway shouldn't be involved in policy making. Furthermore, they believe that government officials with no health care experience really know better than the folks actually on the front line of health care delivery. My experience with John always has been positive and I must say that every chance he has to promote injury prevention and health care cost containment, he seizes. I have sincerely valued his contributions over the years.

John had a role in Bob Dole's campaign in 1996. During that period, he and I participated in a meeting at the Dole headquarters about the issue of prevention and its economic ramifications. The individuals I met there and spoke with seemed incredibly clueless about these issues. Even though we took the horse to water, the horse not only refused to drink, but also kept running away (actually, stampeded away) in the opposite direction. The vision that I saw in Lee Atwater back in the late 1980s had not found a home in the Republican party of the 1990s and has yet to reassert itself.

In one of my meetings at the White House during February 1992, I had a discussion with several folks in the Domestic Policy Council and the Economic Policy Council about the upcoming election campaign. They felt that Bill Clinton would be the nominee and that this would be good for George Bush because Bill Clinton surely could not beat George Bush. After all, George Bush had just led a very successful Persian Gulf War campaign and Bill Clinton just had too much in his past. I think I shocked and surprised some of these individuals by saying that I felt Bill Clinton had developed a connection with the American public, and that they should be careful for what they wished. Although I didn't agree with Bill Clinton on many things, I did feel he had charisma and a vision that connected with the American public, and he could well prove an extremely formidable force.

That was the last time I ever attended a meeting in the White House. I was not asked back and didn't hear from the White House until the day after Bill Clinton was elected president in November

1992. As one of his last actions, President Bush did appoint me to the Advisory Board for the newly created National Center for Injury Prevention and Control, a board that addresses injury prevention and health care cost containment issues. The Center funds injury prevention research and brings these issues to the public's attention. I felt it a great honor that President Bush and Secretary of Health and Human Services Dr. Louis Sullivan selected me for this prestigious position. I also served on the Center for Disease Control Grant Review Committee. Under the Clinton administration, I was appointed to the National Institute of Health Trauma Research Task Force and the International Collaborative Effort on Injury Prevention and Control. I served as a delegate to the latter group, which focused on international injury and prevention issues. I enjoyed all of my time on these boards and I felt that at the conclusion of my service we had furthered the cause of injury and sports injury prevention. We increased awareness of the economic consequences of injury and the role of prevention as well as increased research done on injury and injury prevention.

My foray into the government arena also led me to encounter the governor of the state of Michigan, John Engler. Mr. Engler has a long-standing, very positive relationship with the health care community, and Congressman Purcell asked me to attend several meetings that the governor also attended. On these occasions, I spoke with Governor Engler about injury prevention and he seemed very interested in integrating our ideas on injury prevention with health care cost containment initiatives in Michigan. I found his interest to be very reassuring. However, when after two or three or four meetings, I heard the same words and nothing happened, I resolved to say something about it. The next time I met Governor Engler, he again said he would like us to get involved with the state's health care initiatives. I told him, to the astonishment of my wife:

"Governor, I'm tired of all this talk. Your staff does not follow up and does not call. So either you have one of the worse staffs in state government, or you're not delivering the message to your staff and this is all just talk."

My words took the governor aback and Libby turned an incredible crimson shade. But I felt that if we were going to get the ball down the field any further, someone had to confront the coach about things not going well. His mouth fell open and no words were spoken. An aide then hurriedly came to his side and ushered him off. My comments seemed to have an impact. Shortly after our conversation, I received a call from one of Governor Engler's staff members. He invited me to become the sole physician member of the Governor's Council on Health, Fitness, and Sports. Over the next five years, I had the wonderful opportunity to serve with many dedicated people appointed by the governor, in particular, Dr. Karen Pettersmarck, Mr. Tom Johnson, Mr. Jan Christensen, and Charles Kunzelman, chairman of the Governor's Council.

The Governor's Council had a significant and positive effect on the Michigan populace, by increasing awareness of injury and injury prevention. The council also developed a curriculum program for physical fitness in Michigan schools and a funding program, through the cigarette tax Governor Engler initiated, to address physical fitness and health education issues. In fact, the council had a significant impact nationally, serving as a model for several governors' councils around the United States. Governor Engler also appointed me chairman of the Sports Injury Advisory Group, where again I had the fortunate opportunity of serving with Dr. Karen Pettersmarck. We worked together with an advisory group that developed handbooks on preventing injuries in sports such as football, soccer, and inline skating. So despite our early encounters, Governor Engler proved to not only talk the talk, but also walk the walk for prevention of sports injuries. He has since become the strongest gubernatorial advocate in the nation for injury prevention.

I have met many wonderful people over the years during my travels to and from Washington. My most memorable meeting occurred on a flight following the dedication of the Holocaust Museum in Washington. On the flight back from National Airport, I sat next to an elderly couple traveling to Detroit en route to their home in Montreal. They asked me why I had been to Washington. I told them that I was there to talk with government officials about health care and injury prevention; I wasn't sure that these officials listened, but at least I had an opportunity to address injury prevention.

I asked the couple why they had been to Washington. The man said that they went to the dedication of the Holocaust Museum. I asked him about the dedication and he said that he found it one of the most difficult experiences he had had, probably only second to his confinement in the concentration camp at Auschwitz. With that, his wife held up her hand.

"Don't talk any further," she told him.

"No," he responded, "I think it's important for us to talk to people, especially younger people, about what happened so that history never repeats itself." He rolled up his sleeve and showed me a number that had been tattooed on his forearm. "For several years I lost my identity," he said. "And this is all I was." Then he rolled up his wife's sleeve and showed me her identifying number. "If you remember anything of our conversation," he told me, "remember these two tattoos. Remember that people should not be reduced to a tattooed number on their forearm, that every individual matters, and the more individuals you can help singly and collectively, the better life you will have and the better life you will create for others." It was a lesson to never forget, and on long, tough days, I still hear his voice and his story—it inspires me!

The elderly couple went on to tell me stories of their imprisonment, the death of their 15 family members (they were the only two survivors in their respective families), and the day that troops liberated them just as the older gentleman lay dying of typhoid fever. This very moving encounter with these wonderfully gracious people became one of the greatest educational moments I ever experienced.

On a lighter note, after another Washington trip in which I had been fairly blunt, actually brutally blunt with representatives of the Clinton administration about their handling of health care related issues, I arrived in Detroit fairly late in the evening. As I walked through the airport, I noticed somebody following me. I made a stop at the bathroom only to realize that this person followed me into the bathroom. He continued to follow me to the baggage claim area. I stood there waiting for my baggage and this individual walked up to me. I wasn't sure who he was and felt a little nervous. I thought maybe one of the Clintonistas had followed me because of my rather vocal criticism of the Clinton administration in a fairly large public forum. I thought maybe they wanted to talk to me about my candor. The individual walked up to me and said, "I know who you are."

"No you don't," I told him.

"Yes I do," he said.

Then I asked him, "Who do you think I am?"

"You're Bill Gates."

Now I must admit, I do look a bit like Bill Gates. I'm about $250 billion shy of his bank account. But since that time, folks will come up to me maybe two, three, or four times a week and ask if I'm Bill Gates. When I say no, I usually get the same response as

I got from this gentleman at the baggage claim. I told him I wasn't Bill Gates, and he insisted I was and even asked me to show him my driver's license. I handed it to him. He looked it over and said, "Mr. Gates, with your money, you can afford to be anybody you want to be. I know who you are, and there's nothing you can do to convince me that you're not Bill Gates." Then he said, "Can I ask you a question?"

"Sure," I said.

"Mr. Gates", he asked. "Why do you fly coach on Northwest Airlines when you're a multibillionaire? Why would you fly coach on Northwest Airlines eating peanuts?"

"So I can't convince you I'm not Bill Gates, right?" I said.

And he said, "No, you can't."

"All right. I have a fair amount of money, don't I?"

"Mr. Gates," he said. "You have billions of dollars."

"O.K.," I said, "Do you know how you get billions of dollars?" And with this, the gentleman launched into a dissertation about developing a software platform and developing this and that. I stopped him after he had gone on for several minutes and said, "You know, you're right, that's part of it, but let me give you a little hint. It's not how much you make, it's how much you save, and do you know how much money you save flying coach on Northwest Airlines eating peanuts?"

The gentleman grinned and said, "Wow! Thank you!" And with that, he shook my hand and wandered off. So somewhere around the United States someone thinks that Bill Gates flies coach on Northwest Airlines and eats peanuts. This was my first Bill Gates sighting. Ever since, at least three or four times a week, some one asks me if I'm Bill Gates. This has happened at golf courses, gas stations, grocery stores, clothing stores, resorts, and restaurants. It's usually a telltale sign that folks think I'm Bill Gates when we see people pointing in restaurants. The second clue is when the maitre d' or the owner or the waitress or the waiter bring us free hors d'oeuvres and free desserts and thanks us for coming to their restaurant.

This identity confusion seems to run in the family. Not infrequently, folks confuse Libby with Helen Hunt, the Oscar and Emmy-winning actress (although not as frequently as they confuse me with Bill Gates). One spring, Libby and I and our two kids, Allison and Katie, vacationed in Bermuda. We stayed at a nice resort and at the restaurant one night, we saw people pointing at us. Shortly thereafter, a waitress brought over a plate of appetizers. "Compliments of the house," she told us.

Libby leaned over and whispered to me, "Is it the Bill Gates thing or the Helen Hunt thing?"

"I don't know," I whispered back. "Let's see what happens."

About ten minutes later the waitress came over to Libby and asked her, "Ma'am, has anyone ever told you that you look like Helen Hunt?"

"Yes, I've heard that," responded Libby.

And the waitress looked at her and said, "Well, are you?"

Libby told her no, but for the rest of the dinner, people kept pointing at us, and the waitress brought over some desserts for the kids, compliments of the house. After dinner, the girls and Lib headed back to the room and I headed to the lobby because we planned to check out the next morning. As I walked through the lobby, a fellow grabbed my arm and asked me, "Sir, how was your stay?"

"It was fine," I told him.

"We take pride that folks have a relaxing stay at our resort and that it's a hassle-free resort for our celebrity guests," he told me.

I looked at him and asked, "Who do you think our family is?"

"Well sir, I know that you are going under the name of Janda, but I know your real identity."

I asked, "Who am I?"

"Why, you're Bill Gates," he said.

"Let me show you my driver's license," I told him.

"Sir, I can imagine you have a driver's license that says you are Mr. Janda, and as far as we're concerned, fine, you're Mr. Janda, but I hope that when you get back home you'll tell some of your friends that you had a nice stay at our resort."

"What can I do to convince you I'm not Bill Gates?"

"Nothing sir," he said. "But could I ask you a question?" I thought he was going to ask me for an autograph. Now, the one thing I don't do when folks mistake me for Bill Gates is sign autographs. I usually just say that Bill Gates doesn't sign autographs. Many folks have asked to take a picture, and I tell them, "As long as you understand I'm not Bill Gates, fine, take a picture." But this gentleman didn't ask me for an autograph or a photo. Instead he asked, "How long have you been seeing Helen Hunt?"

I told him, "Well, I'll tell you what. Let's just keep this between the two of us. Just pretend that I wasn't here with Helen Hunt."

"Your secret is safe with me," he told me.

So somewhere along the line if the *National Enquirer* or *The Star* or some such tabloid prints a story about folks seeing Bill Gates hanging out with Helen Hunt, we all know where they got the story.

CHAPTER SEVEN

Not All that Glitters is Gold

"Take nothing on its looks, take everything on evidence. There is no better rule."

—CHARLES DICKENS

Our airways and newspapers are filled with stories of the heroics and great feats accomplished in the sports world. In recognition of these great accomplishments, we reward our athletes with medals, plaques, and money. But not all that glitters in the sports world is gold, particularly with the players behind the scenes such as the sporting goods industry. In our encounters with the industry, we were soon to discover the truth of the old saws "Buyer beware" and "Don't believe everything you read or hear in the media."

After we published our breakaway base studies, reporters from CNN, ABC, NBC, CBS, Associated Press, USA Today and other major news organizations started calling our office regularly to write about injury prevention. It wasn't long before I started to hear about other serious baseball injuries from parents and coaches who had seen or heard their stories. Several parents from Tampa Bay called me about an incident where a child playing baseball died when a pitched ball struck him in the chest. The parents researched this event on the Internet and found this wasn't an isolated incident; several children had died after a ball hit them in the chest during games. Several reporters also called me to ask about this incident. About this time, I ran into Dr. Theo Polley, a pediatric general surgeon at the University of Michigan, who had just begun to investigate these injuries. He suggested that with my expertise in sports injuries, I should look into these incidents as well.

So I contacted the Consumer Product Safety Commission (CPSC) and asked for information on fatalities due to chest impact with a baseball. The next week, I received an article from the CPSC reviewing chest-impact fatalities in baseball. The article, written three years earlier, discussed a phenomenon called the "chest-impact fatality scenario" in baseball, hockey and lacrosse. The article noted that roughly two children a year (ages 5-14) died, that they knew about, after baseballs struck them in the chest. Furthermore, this was the most common cause of death among children playing sports.

The article didn't identify how the impact caused the children's death nor did it have any further research demonstrating the medical reason for these deaths. We reviewed the medical literature extensively and found no discussion of chest impact fatalities in baseball. Our literature search did reveal that the automotive industry had done most of the research on blunt impact to the chest leading to injury or fatality.

I spoke with Dr. Polley about our literature search and he told me that he knew researchers in the automotive industry and that I should call Dr. David Viano, the principal research scientist at General Motors Research Laboratories in Warren, Michigan. With guarded optimism, having experienced hundreds of "No's" from corporate America, I called David Viano. I told Dr. Vivano about our interest in chest impact research, and asked if the General Motors research team would work with us in studying baseball chest-impact injuries.

Now, many companies talk about prevention, but when push comes to shove, they never come through. I must say Dave Viano and General Motors proved very open to working with the Institute and investigating sports fatalities occurring to youth in our country. I felt this to be a milestone in our development, with GM enthusiastically coming on board. I knew it would make a difference.

General Motors had been interested primarily in investigating air bag deployment. Their interest stemmed from reports that several people, in particular, elderly and young folks, had died when deployed air bags hit them in the chest. At that time, collisions caused canister-shaped air bags to deploy and hit the chest at high speeds. The General Motors research team investigated this phenomenon and found that if a projectile hit the chest at a precise phase in the heart cycle, it could short-circuit the heart and produce a rapidly beating heart that could lead to death. Dr. Viano thought that this could well be the cause of children's deaths on baseball fields.

We decided to take the same approach we had taken with breakaway bases and investigate sports equipment that might prevent these deaths. So we contacted the sports equipment industry and asked about products that might prevent or reduce chest impact fatalities. We found that manufacturers promoted two types of products as injury prevention devices, softer baseballs and chest protectors.

The major proponent of the softer baseball, the Worth Sports Company, recently had distributed a multipage advertisement promoting softer baseballs. The ad noted that 51 baseball-related deaths occurred over a 10-year period. Most of the victims were children and most of these children died after a baseball struck them in the chest. The ad went on to list four children's names, their ages, and the dates that they died. The ad further implied that using the Worth's Reduced Injury Factor baseball (RIF) would save the lives of children, and that if the RIF ball had been used, the four children cited in the advertisement would be alive today. At this point I was encouraged by what I read.

The other product touted by manufacturers as an injury prevention device was a chest protector for batters and pitchers. One prominent chest protector manufacturer, the International Protective Athletic Safety Corporation, distributed a multipage color advertisement that stated the following:

"Lightweight, durable, and highly effective, the athletic safety jacket helps to reduce injuries and prevent deaths for batters and fielders alike, while restoring confidence in athletic ability for better performance." Again, I was hopeful.

At first, we held hope for products such as the IPASC vest and the Worth softer baseball. Despite the hyperbole found in their advertisements, we hoped they were right that these products might offer some benefit to young athletes.

Before we began the testing, we spent several months contacting several softer baseball and chest protector manufacturers and asked them to supply us with data or published studies on their products. None would comply. We thought perhaps they had not forwarded their studies to us simply because we sent our requests to the wrong people. But it soon became apparent that none of these companies had the data or science to support their marketing claims. Unfortunately, the marketing of health or prevention benefits without substantiation appears to be a fairly common practice with companies in the sporting goods industry.

So with no studies to investigate, we decided to proceed with our own research on the prevention of chest impact injuries. We broke this research into several phases. During the first phase, Dave Viano and his research team performed very limited animal model testing at the General Motors Research Laboratories. A multidisciplinary team, from the Institute and G.M., of physiologists, veterinarians, biomechanical engineers, orthopedic surgeons, and cardiologists worked on this series of studies. Veterinarians and physiologists told us that a pig's chest structure best mimicked a child's. A child's chest structure is less rigid than an adult's and thus more prone to chest impact fatality. So we conducted our tests using a limited number of pigs under strict NIH guidelines for humane treatment. We found in this series of tests that if the baseball impacted the heart or the chest at the precise phase of the heart and breathing cycle, that it short-circuited the heart. This made the heart beat wildly, so wildly that the heart could not pump blood effectively to the vital organs, and the animal died. This study confirmed previous testing done in the automotive industry with air bags. We also found cardiac arrhythmia results very similar to those documented on baseball fields when paramedics arrived on the scene to treat children struck in the chest with a baseball.

Now, it is important to put this in perspective. Millions of children play youth baseball every year. They are hit by both pitched balls and batted balls millions of times. Roughly two children a year die from these impacts. Now, granted, this is not an epidemic. On the other hand, these kids are not playing with hand grenades, and, obviously, one death is one too many.

Many people have said to us, "Well, you know, it's only two kids a year." But we all know that if it's your child, or your grandchild, or your niece or your nephew or your neighbor or a member of your community, it's a significant tragedy. One child dying a year playing a sport is one too many, and we need to prevent such tragedies.

During the study, we found that if you give a thump to the chest immediately after impact occurs, you can break the arrhythmia and the animal has a higher chance of survival. The American Heart Association had removed the pre-cordial thump, or thump to the chest, from its list of approved CPR techniques. But we believe that when chest impact occurs and a child collapses, a thump to the chest is probably the best and most effective initial action you can take. Better yet, an automated external defibrillator (AED) can monitor the rhythm and deliver a shock to the heart. Such action can help bring the heart from arrhythmia back into a normal beat pattern.

The second positive benefit of the animal testing was that it allowed us to correlate live studies with the automotive industry's Hybrid 3 crash model dummy, which became the gold standard for chest impact research testing. You've seen the crash dummies in seatbelt public service announcements on TV. But the Hybrid 3 crash model isn't just a dummy, it's a very sophisticated computerized device with sensors that can measure the force of impact, the moment of the impact, and how long the impact occurs. The sensors also measure how far the chest caves in and how fast it caves in when the impact occurs. This measurement of how fast the chest caves in and how much it caves in, called the Viscous Criterion, provides the most sensitive indication of the risk of injury. I consider General Motors development of this testing dummy a major breakthrough for not only the automobile industry but now for the sports industry.

Unfortunately, a controversy soon arose over our use of limited animal testing in this phase of the study. Animal rights activists read media reports about the research and phoned in threats to bomb the lab at General Motors. I spoke with some of these individuals because I wanted them to know we understood their concerns and explained that we carefully followed the strict

NIH guidelines for humane and ethical treatment of animals. Furthermore, we had used a limited number of animals in the initial phase of the study and no longer were using them. The data we obtained from the animal testing allowed us to change over to a computerized model, the Hybrid 3 crash model, and we no longer needed to do animal testing. Furthermore, because we correlated the data from our animal testing with the Hybrid 3 crash model, we undoubtedly saved hundreds, if not thousands, of animals in the long run; researchers could now use crash dummy models to replace animal models.

One activist told me that, "If we want to find out what's happening to children, we should use children in the testing." I angrily asked this individual if he would be willing to volunteer his child. Of course, he said, "no." I asked who would he suggest, and which parent I should call to donate their child for this particular study. He had no answer. Animal testing is a difficult question. I value life in every shape and form and, as a physician, I was trained to preserve life. But I believe that we treated the animals used in this study in a humane manner and that the testing led to significant findings and savings of human and animal life, and that's a trade-off I'd make again if required.

After we completed the first phase of our study and found the mechanism that led to these children's death, i.e., cardiac arrhythmia from chest impact, we began to test the currently available prevention products. First we obtained standard hard baseballs used in youth leagues throughout the United States. We next obtained several types of softer baseballs with which to compare them. We also obtained several of the vests touted as preventative devices.

Many of the companies that make these products willingly provided samples for testing. Others proved more hesitant. I remember one conversation, in particular, with Sam Marion, the owner of the International Protective Athletic Safety Corporation. I asked him if he would send his chest protector and told him that we would be happy to test the product free of charge and compare it to other types of protectors as well as to the unprotected chest. He asked me, " If you show that our product does not help, will you still publish the results?" I told him yes and Mr. Marion said he would not send us a test product. Unfortunately, his was not the only such response; several other companies refused to send their products because we could not guarantee positive test results. Indeed, the results weren't positive for many of the products we tested.

We also contacted several of the softer baseball manufacturers, including Jess Heald, a principal in the Worth Corporation. He sent us some of the Worth softer baseballs to test, and actually visited the General Motors research labs with several members of his staff to review the testing. Our relationship with Worth and the other manufacturers seemed cordial at this time, although I had the distinct impression that some of them felt uneasy about an independent scientific organization investigating their products, particularly when we refused to accept any funding from the industry.

So we began our testing using the standard hard baseball as the control. We measured the force, momentum, and duration of baseball impacts at different speeds on the Hybrid 3 crash dummy. We also measured the most sensitive indicator of the risk of injury, i.e., the depth of the baseball's penetration into the chest upon impact and the speed at which the chest caved in.

To make a long story short, we found both the softer baseballs and the chest protectors afforded no significant protection. In fact, shockingly, some of the softer baseballs and some of the chest protectors actually increased the risk of injury.

Our research team repeated the study again and again to see if the results actually held up over time. Every time, the results came out the same. At first, we found it difficult to explain why these supposedly safer products actually made the problem worse. Our results seemed contrary to common sense. Why would a softer baseball or a chest protector actually produce a greater risk of injury? The answer becomes clear when you more closely examine a baseball. Softness and hardness are only one of a ball's features, and these are only surface features. These features have nothing to do with the weight or mass or the properties of material used to construct the ball. We found these to be more critical qualities affecting impact. In fact, when we measured and weighed the softer baseballs, we found that many of them weighed more than the standard hard baseball. So despite their relative softness, some of the softer baseballs proved heavier and hit the chest with greater impact than a standard hardball.

We also reviewed our high-speed photographic work and found that when softer, heavier baseballs hit the chest, the ball stuck to the chest for a greater length of the time than the standard baseball. So, the softer, heavier baseball hit the chest, stuck to the chest for a longer period of time, and drove into the heart with more force and energy than the standard baseball. This is crucial because of the less well-developed chest structure in children. Furthermore, when it pushed off, the softer baseball actually rebounded with more force.

Our studies correlated with military research on softer shell casings. These studies found that softer shells stuck to armor for a longer period of time than ordinary casings and this allowed the backside of a shell to pierce the armor. We contacted some folks in the military and they confirmed that shells coated in the softer material with a softer nose cone actually increased the impact and made the projectile more lethal. When we told them of what we thought were surprising findings with the baseball, they weren't surprised at all, as they knew this principle for years.

We also investigated several chest protectors that were to be worn by batters and pitchers. These are not the same type of protection that catchers wear. The idea of using chest protectors isn't bad. Again, it seems intuitive that a chest protector would reduce the force of a baseball hitting the chest. However, the protection afforded depends on the type of material used in the chest protector. All of the chest protectors we tested consisted of a closed-cell foam type of material. The foam acted like a conductor, and actually drove the energy of the baseball into the heart with more force than with an unprotected chest.

We videotaped and recorded all of our findings and presented these findings to a group of scientists at the Institute and a scientific review board at General Motors. We also sent this information to the Consumer Products Safety Commission (CPSC). After several months of review, Dr. Bob Verhalen, Associate Director of the CPSC told us that he and others at the Consumer Products Safety Commission agreed with our procedures, our findings, and our conclusions. Dr. Verhalen told us that he thought it extremely important to inform the public about our findings and encouraged us to send our studies to a peer-reviewed medical journal for publication. This encouraged both David Viano and me to chart the next course. So we submitted our series of studies to the Clinical Journal of Sport Medicine (CJSM), a prestigious international journal in sports medicine. The CJSM accepted our study and published it in early 1992.

In addition to our findings on softer baseballs and chest protectors, our article noted a common denominator in these incidents appeared to be that children essentially panicked and walked into pitches. A trained player approaches a pitch somewhat differently. Watch Cal Ripken bat. When the ball comes at him, he actually turns his body away and tucks his head. So the ball hits him in between or on his scapula, i.e., the wing-bone in the back. Unfortunately, the children killed in these incidents never received any formal training in how to get out of the way of the pitch. They were like "a deer in the highlights." Consequently, instead of turning away, they walked into the pitch. So we recommended that children receive training in how to avoid being hit by a pitch. Our study concluded that promoting the current products on the market as safer creates a false sense of security. Until better products are developed, more adequate training and coaching remain the keys to preventing these injuries.

Despite the scientific nature of our findings, some in the sporting goods industry didn't welcome our results. This became clear after the first media reports of our findings began to appear. Joe Garagiola and his producer, Ginny Seipt from the "Today Show" produced one of the first stories. They brought the "Today Show" crew to the Institute and to the General Motors' research labs and spent three days conducting interviews with Dr. Viano and me as well as several members of the research team.

Shortly after the story appeared in late May 1992, we received several phone calls from parents and coaches asking us to forward our studies to them so they could review the results, and take the necessary steps to safeguard their community. We also received phone calls from some industry representatives who seemed genuinely concerned, in particular, the Rawlings and Wilson Corporations. They noted they had read the study and wanted to know what they could do to make softer baseballs better. Both these manufacturers had developed softer baseball products, primarily in response to the marketing efforts of the Worth Company. Neither had promoted these products heavily because they doubted their effectiveness. Our study confirmed their suspicions. Both manufacturers asked for suggestions in improving the product and I told them they needed to change the materials they used and make the softer baseballs lighter.

Other responses to our story weren't as positive. Less than a week after the "Today Show" broadcast the story, the producers received a threatening letter from David A. Maxon, a technical consultant with the IPASC Corporation. His letter said that the story had libeled chest protectors and that the "Today Show" story producers would have "blood on their hands" if another child died from chest impact while not wearing a chest protector.

The Institute also began to receive threatening phone calls suggesting that we obtain liability insurance. The individuals making the calls identified themselves as representatives of the Rawlings Corporation. I found this conversation strange, given that the Rawlings Corporation had just called me and asked for suggestions on improving baseball products. So I called Jim Conley from the Rawlings Corporation and asked him about the calls. He assured me that no one at Rawlings would make such a call to the Institute and told me he would investigate. He called back two days latter and suggested that possibly someone at the IPASC Corporation had made the call.

Not 10 minutes after the first threatening phone call, Bill Laitner, a reporter from the *Detroit Free Press*, called and told us he had just received a rude and accusatory phone call from the IPASC Corporation. Mr. Laitner had run an article in the *Free Press* about the "Today Show" story. The IPASC Corporation representative suggested to Mr. Laitner that IPASC competitors had bribed the Institute.

At this point, I asked Libby, a practicing attorney as I mentioned before, to find out more about Mr. Maxon. The letter he wrote to the "Today Show" contained much legal jargon and I felt he could well have a legal background. Libby did an attorney discipline board search and found that Mr. Maxon had been suspended from the Michigan State Bar on several occasions, specifically for failing to adequately represent his clients and for charging excessive fees. I found it interesting that an individual with his background would make allegations of corruption and bribery about a nonprofit, independent, scientific research organization that refused to accept any money from the sporting goods industry. Fortunately, NBC and the "Today Show" dismissed Mr. Maxon's allegations and, with the help of my wife and her law firm, we contacted Mr. Maxon and demanded that he stop making false allegations and misrepresentations to the press and the public.

Jess Heald and the Worth Corporation launched the second attack on our research. One evening at home, just after our research was published, I received a phone call from an individual who had attended a Worth Corporation sales meeting arranged by Mr. Heald, the company president. At the meeting, Heald passed out a memo to the sales representatives completely misrepresenting the Institute's chest impact study and impugning our motives by suggesting that we were out to "grab headlines." Furthermore, it criticized General Motors involvement with the study and said they should stick to testing air bags and stay out of testing sports equipment. In matters of fact, the memo completely ignored our findings that some softer baseballs are heavier and hit the chest with greater impact than a standard hardball. Instead, it implied that our results weren't relevant for the lower speeds at which baseballs are pitched in youth leagues (sheer nonsense, since the speed only affects the incidence of injury, not the mechanism of injury). Interestingly, prior to publication of our findings, Mr. Heald supported our work. In fact, he had published a 1991 advertisement (of which we were completely unaware) stating that the Worth Corporation was working with the Institute to determine the potential safety benefits of their softer baseballs in preventing children's deaths from chest impact.

When he previously visited the General Motors' research labs, Mr. Heald was gracious and full of Southern charm, though I wondered how much was contrived. We offered him the preliminary results of our studies before they were published and asked if he or his team had any criticism or comments. He said no. But after the studies were published, he began and continues to this day to distribute literature that misrepresented our study in every respect. The individual who contacted me said that he felt taken aback by Mr. Heald's approach and found him to be more of a zealot than a reasonable individual looking out for the public welfare. He also said that what bothered him the most was that Mr. Heald cloaked himself in a mantel of prevention, but actually only seemed concerned about market share and the economic welfare of his company and himself. He felt he did not really care about the truth or the science of the matter and what could ultimately benefit the youth of America.

Rather than attempt to address the problem, Mr. Heald and the Worth Company spent millions of dollars in marketing the softer, heavier baseball and in attempting to convince sports organizations to endorse his softer baseball. Much of this money was spent on misleading advertising such as the ad that listed the names of children who had died after being hit in the chest with a baseball (implying that if their teams had used softer baseballs, these children could well be alive today).

In a deposition regarding a chest impact fatality, under oath, Mr. Heald was asked whether Worth had tested any of its softer baseballs in relation to chest impact. He responded, "No". Yet, if you read the company's publicly circulated advertisements, they gave the impression that Worth had thoroughly tested their products and found them safe.

Mr. Heald also attempted to cloak their claims in the mantel of the National Operating Committee for the Safety of Athletic Equipment (NOCSAE), an organization funded by the sporting goods manufacturers to test equipment and develop standards. The committee had adopted a standard that Worth claimed had proved the RIF product effective. The Wilson Corporation, the other manufacturer that had contacted us after our studies were published asking for advice in improving their products, sent us two letters addressing this issue. The first letter outlined how, "as NOCSAE's work on this standard progressed, a close relationship developed between NOCSAE's testing and safety standard supervisor and the president of the Worth Company. Subsequently NOCSAE's ensuing reports began to refer to the entire category of softer balls, not in a generic sense, but using Worth's trademark name for its softer ball products 'RIF' (for 'Reduced Injury Factor' baseballs)." Over time, Wilson and other manufacturers began to privately question the independence and credibility of NOCSAE's tests and reports. Such questions led Wilson, which sat on NOCSAE's ad hoc safety committee throughout the 1980s, to reduce, and in 1990, eliminate its participation on the committee. The credibility of NOCSAE in this one area remains an issue of contention among representatives of manufacturers at the Sporting Goods Manufacturer's Association meetings.

Wilson and other manufacturers submitted letters questioning NOCSAE's testing procedures and prescribed safety standards and, in particular, expressed concern over the lack of applicability of NOCSAE standards to body-chest impacts. "Wilson can state it has never received a substantive response to its concerns," according to the letter we received. The letter further stated that Worth, "has directly acknowledged the lack of safety evidence related to chest and body impacts from softer, more compressible balls. In view of the potential for a misunderstanding by the public, the Institute deserves great credit for bringing the chest impact issue to light. A ball should not be marketed as safer, if such marketing might reasonably lead the public to assume a safety benefit (on chest impacts) which is not known to exist."

We found the response of manufacturers such as Wilson and Rawlings to our research enlightening; it suggests that some sporting goods manufacturers are interested in doing what is right for the public rather than simply making more money at the expense of the public.

In 1991, the Worth Company distributed promotional literature calling for funds to be appropriated for research on baseball and chest impact deaths in children. But not too long after, the Worth Corporation sent a threatening letter to General Motors demanding that GM stop our research effort. The letter further asked the vice president in charge of General Motors' research labs to "refrain from further public disclosure" about our research studies. Robert Frosch, the vice president of General Motors research labs, responded to Mr. Heald and told him that Dr. Viano would continue to pursue studies on baseball injury risk and prevention and would continue his relationship with the Institute for Preventative Sports Medicine. I find it hypocritical that Mr. Heald told the public that his company encourages preventative research, yet does everything in his power to misrepresent and squash preventative studies that will benefit the public.

Mr. Heald's letter did have one negative effect. It led General Motors' legal department to suspend a public education campaign it had planned to inform the public about the dangers of baseball chest impacts and how these might be prevented. As a result, the public, once again, failed to receive important information about the risk of chest impact fatalities occurring in baseball. Furthermore, the Worth advertising campaign, or rather misinformation campaign, has exposed millions of children to continued risk from these injuries. Unethical business practices such as those practiced by Worth harm the public in a stealth manner. Their misinformation campaign allows more children to become potential victims.

Obviously Worth can disagree with our findings. But then the onus is on them to produce legitimate independent scientific research on the issue and have it peer-reviewed and published in the medical literature. In the meantime, until contradictory findings are published, they have the responsibility to warn people of the potential risks of softer, heavier baseballs. As of today, Mr. Heald and the Worth Corporation have failed to produce any peer-reviewed independent scientific studies that contradict our findings nor have they warned the public about the potential problems with their products. I have only one question about this. Auto companies are required to recall defective and unsafe auto products. Why aren't sporting goods manufacturers subject to the same standards? Ralph Nader once wrote a book about automotive safety called, *Unsafe at Any Speed*. This seems an appropriate epithet for softer baseballs as well.

After our series of studies were published, some coaches and league officials suggested we recommend at least one of the chest protectors or one of the softer baseballs, since "some obviously were better than others." However, we knew from our tests that none were better than any of the others. None of these products reduced the potential risk of fatality and injury from baseball chest impacts to a statistically significant degree. So we could not recommend any of them. Others suggested we look at the issue of head impact as well as the chest impact from baseballs.

So we began two new research studies, the first looking at the head impact issue, and the second looking at some of the newer products aimed at reducing chest impact fatalities. St. Joseph's Mercy Hospital funded the study and gave us space for a lab on its campus. Using the Hybrid 3 crash model system in this series of studies, we found that a lighter-mass baseball is more effective in preventing chest impact injuries than a softer, heavier baseball. We also found that in chest impacts at speeds of 40 and 50 and 60 miles per hour, the softer, heavier baseballs in some instances increased the risk of injury. The lighter-mass baseballs on all occasions significantly reduced the risk of injury. We also found that lighter-mass baseballs were more effective in reducing the risk of injury for head impacts. However, wearing a helmet with ear and face protection should still provide the most effective protection against injury from head impact.

Recently, manufacturers have touted the findings of Dr. Mark Link, a cardiologist in Boston in his chest impact study. In a series of animal model studies, Dr. Link concluded that the timing of the impact was critical to the development of cardiac arrhythmia. Dr. Link touted this as a new finding, but actually it was noted in GM automotive studies of chest impact in the early 1980s. The GM studies showed that a chest impact that occurred at a precise phase of the cardiac cycle led to a greater incidence of arrhythmia. In addition to confirming these findings, Dr. Link concluded that softer baseballs were effective at reducing the risk of chest impact fatality. His conclusion proved truly unfortunate because when one reviews his study, it's obvious that his findings differed little from ours. He tested three Worth RIF balls and found that two of them led to no statistically significant reduction in the risk of injury or fatality compared to a standard hard baseball. The only softer baseball he tested that he found effectively reduced the risk of injury was the lightest of the three balls he tested. Unfortunately, he never tested the lightest baseballs that are currently on the market.

Furthermore, Dr. Link's study found that even in the case of the lighter weight softer baseball, chest impact led to a fatal arrhythmia 8% of the time. Unfortunately, the press releases on his research suggested that all softer baseballs significantly reduced the risk of fatality or injury and, furthermore, that using softer baseballs produced little to no risk of fatality or injury. I wouldn't call 8% of these impacts causing fatal arrhythmias "little to no risk." Surely the other two softer baseballs, which he found similar in risk to the standard baseball, could not be considered safe to any degree. Unfortunately the publicity surrounding this study only served to further misrepresent the issue to the public. Ironically, at about the time Dr. Link published his study, a child died in Alabama after a softer baseball struck him in the chest. By the way, guess who funded Dr. Link's study? The National Operating Committee for Safety in Athletic Equipment (NOCSAE), an organization funded by the sporting goods manufacturers. Once the data from the field indicated softer baseballs were involved in chest impact deaths, Dr. Link started to change his tune and admitted "a chest wall protective device may not only be ineffective, but increase the likelihood of a fatal impact." A conclusion our team realized 10 years prior to his "revelation". Unfortunately, for 10 years, the public was misled by misrepresentation of our studies. The public was given a false sense of security by his statements and by some of the manufacturers. In 2003, Dr. Link then started to support AED's. All of us welcome him to "the other side." By the way, the study he authored supporting AED's was co-funded by a company manufacturing AED's.

Sadly, other organizations that promote safety in sports for children have gotten caught up in Worth's misinformation campaign. In September 1991, the National Youth Sports Coaches Association (NYSCA), an organization that certifies coaches, held a "Safety in Baseball" summit in Orlando, Florida. By certifying coaches, the NYSCA provides a significant benefit to young athletes throughout the country; the certification process ensures that coaches teach the fundamentals, and knowing the fundamentals is one of the best methods to avoid injury. So when they asked me to present our research on breakaway bases as well as on the chest impact scenario, I said yes without hesitation. I didn't realize at the time that Worth was a sponsor of the event. I attended the summit and presented our findings to polite applause. Immediately following the summit, I returned home. Shortly thereafter, I received a call from Mike Pfahl, an NYSCA official. He was preparing a written summary of the meeting and asked if he could say that the Institute gave a qualified recommendation on the use of softer baseballs. I was shocked. I told him that this contradicted our findings and that I could not make such a statement to the public since it truly misrepresented our findings. Our findings were that softer, heavier baseballs were not effective.

This case in point illustrates why the Institute adopted the rule that we will never accept money from the sporting goods industry. Unfortunately, money can color and taint organizations and individuals, and in this case, I believe that accepting Worth's money led an organization committed to safety in sports into potentially acting against its own principles. This can happen with private organizations, and it can happen with governmental bodies, as we were soon to discover with the Consumer Product Safety Commission.

Ann Brown, the CPSC chair, contacted me in August 1994 and invited David Viano and me to participate in a roundtable discussion on baseball protective equipment scheduled in October. Other participants included manufacturers and retailers, consumer advocates, various researchers, folks from the legal community, the medical community, and the sports community. David and I were hopeful and enthusiastic about the opportunity to present our work.

In October, David and I flew to Washington. The flight down gave us extra time to discuss our presentations. We arrived that evening and took a taxi to the hotel. The next morning, another taxi took us to our meeting. The taxi let us off in front of a nondescript, sandstone building and we were ushered up to a large meeting room where tables had been pushed together in a large square. We sat and waited for Ms. Brown. She opened the meeting with a brief statement of the problem and immediately left the room. The roundtable discussion went on for several hours, but she wasn't there to hear any of it. Several researchers presented their findings, including ourselves. By the end of the meeting, we came to a consensus that none of the products currently on the market clearly reduced the risk of chest impact fatalities. As we finished our discussion, Ms. Brown returned and gave her concluding remarks.

Following Ms. Brown's remarks, I left. But while I waited for a cab to take me to the airport, I ran into several manufacturers and consumer advocates who were at the meeting. They had just come from a hastily convened unofficial meeting with Ms. Brown. She had some of her minions pull the manufacturers aside and proceeded to tell them she felt softer baseballs were effective and she wanted them used in baseball leagues. I was horrified since she had not remained in the room to hear the research presented on this matter. Why did the CPSC and specifically Ms. Brown ignore the scientific evidence and trust the marketing hype? Remember, this is the same government agency that supported us presenting this information to the public five years prior to this meeting. Then again, it was a different administration with a different agenda and a different set of values and ethics. Interestingly, the Worth Company is a rather prominent Tennessee based company and some have suggested that they have significant ties to a number of prominent politicians representing Tennessee. Could pressure have been applied here? We will never know, but eventually, in a public statement issued two years later, the CPSC did recommend the use of softer baseballs.

The CPSC public statement in 1996 essentially dismissed our studies and those of other independent scientific researchers. I found this amazing, considering that the CPSC had originally encouraged us to publish our studies and felt it important to disseminate our findings to the public. Consequently, I immediately shot off a letter to the Consumer Product Safety Commission. The letter focused on nine concerns, including the following:

1. Several staff individuals at the Consumer Product Safety Commission related to us as early as the summer of 1994 that the Commission planned to recommend softer baseballs two years prior to their published report. This suggested the commission already had made up its mind before the roundtable took place in 1994.

2. We were told as early as 1995 that the CPSC would complete its review of our studies at the end of October of 1995, and we would have several months to "defend ourselves." I found this an interesting choice of words, given that the commission said it wanted to have an open discussion of the problem. Instead, they seem to have already made their decision. By the way, the CPSC finally sent us the review in February 1996, and gave us two weeks to respond, not the several months promised.

3. On several occasions, we asked CPSC staff whether the commission planned to review our head impact studies as well as our chest impact studies. They said no, because, "Your head impact studies support the use of softer baseballs." I found this to

be a rather curious statement, which, incidentally, CPSC staff members repeated on several occasions. In fact, our head impact study showed that softer baseballs had only a minor effect in preventing injuries from head impacts. We found lighter-weight baseballs were more effective in preventing head impact injury and neither was as effective as baseball helmets. Nevertheless, they decided not to review our head impact studies because they felt they supported the use of a product they wanted to promote, i.e., softer baseballs. They decided to review our chest impact studies because they ran counter to the claims of the softer baseball manufacturers. Our chest impact studies questioned the use of the product they wanted to promote. So their objective all along was to support the use of softer baseballs whatever the evidence to the contrary. Even more curious, they rejected our studies outright because we used Hybrid 3 models for our tests. Now, Volvo, GM, the U.S. military, the FBI, the Justice Department, the British military, and the worldwide auto industry all use Hybrid 3 models to test chest impact and consider Hybrid 3 model testing to be the gold standard. And yet the CPSC said that it rejected the Institute's studies because we used these models. It doesn't make sense.

4. CPSC staff informed us that the commission would not review fraudulent advertising by softer baseball companies. Specifically, the Worth ads claimed that softer baseballs provided an unsubstantiated safety benefit. Furthermore, the ad listed the names of children who had died due to chest impact and implied that softer baseballs would have prevented this from happening.

5. CPSC staff also informed us that the commission would not review any of the manufacturers' literature or unpublished data. So unsubstantiated claims by the manufacturers would not be under review, but our data would. Now with whom should the burden of proof lie? With those who make unsubstantiated injury prevention claims or those who present research that refutes those

claims? I think the answer is obvious. Furthermore, why review our data again? We had submitted all of our videotapes from our testing and all of our published data and raw data and our findings and conclusions to the CPSC as early as 1991. After months of review, their representative, Dr. Bob Verhalen, stated that our research was scientifically valid and that the results should be published and disseminated to the public as soon as possible because it would have a significant impact on public health. So why review our data again and not the manufacturers?

6. No representative from the Consumer Product Safety Commission attended the American Society for Testing Materials' International Baseball Symposium in Atlanta on December 6, 1995. The Institute and two other university research groups presented findings at this symposium that suggested softer baseballs increase the potential risk of chest impact injury.

7. The American Society of Mechanical Engineers (ASME) contacted the Institute in early 1996 and asked if the Consumer Product Safety Commission was biased toward softer baseballs. The ASME wanted to pass on information about new testing results to the Consumer Product Safety Commission, but felt the commission "dismissed" them and seemed completely uninterested. The data submitted by the ASME supported our findings that softer baseballs did not reduce injury to a statistically significant level and, in fact, potentially increased the risk of injury.

8. The only chest impact fatality recorded by the Consumer Product Safety Commission in 1995, a child in Alabama who died on Memorial Day weekend, occurred after the child was struck in the chest with a softer baseball. When we confronted the CPSC staff with this fact and asked why this child died, they responded that it was a one in a million event. Furthermore, CPSC staff related to a reporter that the child's death was "an anecdote." I

would hate to have the parents of the child see a statement from a government official that their child's death was "an anecdote."

9. The CPSC staff told me "We can't figure out why you guys are involved in this" Apparently the notion of an independent, nongovernmental organization investigating injury prevention remains foreign to the bureaucratic mind. We believe that private, independent organizations do have a role in evaluating and delivering to the public information about interventions that could reduce or eliminate needless sports injuries.

Accompanying our letter, we sent the Consumer Product Safety Commission our most recent data, which confirmed our previous studies. They did not review the new data. In conclusion, we found that the Consumer Product Safety Commission was, indeed, stepping to the plate on this issue. However, it stepped to the plate with a corked bat. We feel the CPSC has severely compromised itself on this issue, and its independence and findings are tainted. We truly believe that the Consumer Product Safety Commission has misrepresented this issue to the American public and has undoubtedly caused further harm and injury to countless American children that could well have been avoided.

We found state government officials more proactive than federal officials about injury prevention issues. As early as 1991, Michigan State Senator William Faust contacted us about our studies on baseball chest impact as well as our studies on breakaway bases. Senator Faust asked if legislation should be created to mandate preventative interventions. I told him that it is not the job of the government to legislate preventative interventions for the general public. I felt, and still feel, that government can contribute best by holding forums and sponsoring events where these issues are brought to the public so that people can make their own decisions. I believe that the government needs to highlight and bring attention to the issue. I believe that by giving these issues the light of day, the American public will gain the necessary information to make their children, their grandchildren, and their communities safer places to participate in sports. The public will institute the changes in their own communities.

Senator Faust took my suggestion and sponsored a series of hearings in the Michigan State Legislature during the spring of 1991. Unfortunately I could not attend because I was previously scheduled to give a presentation to the international community in Vancouver, British Columbia. Dr. Don Wild, one of the founders of the Institute and a member of our board of directors, stood in for me. He testified on behalf of the Institute and presented our research on baseball chest impact and on breakaway bases and sliding injuries.

After Don presented the Institute's findings on the chest impact and breakaway base issues, a chest protector manufacturer was called to testify. The senators asked him what studies he had done to support his marketing claims that his chest protector would prevent injury to children. He said he tested his product by having a tester throw balls at children wearing chest protectors as they stood against a wall. The chest protector proved effective because "each child survived." This sad response led Don to ask the manufacturer whether any of the parents knew that the manufacturer was using their children as guinea pigs for this "experiment."

We also received a videotape demonstrating the testing done by another chest protector manufacturer. The video showed an individual who was wrapped in tin foil with a chest protector pulled over him. He stood behind a piece of plywood with a two feet by two feet hole cut into it. The tester stuck an arrow in a baseball and shot it through the hole. It was supposed to hit the chest, but the tester made a bad shot and hit the plywood board.

The ball then bounced up and hit the chest protector. The guy came out from behind the piece of plywood and said, "I'm still alive," implying that obviously this chest protector works. The tester removed the chest protector and looked at the dent in the tin foil to see where the impact occurred. This absolute joke of a test is the level of "science" occurring in some manufacturers' labs. These same folks argue the validity of our peer-reviewed research published in the medical literature. Obviously all that glitters is not gold in at least some of the manufacturers' headquarters. In fact, some of their claims seem more like tin.

CHAPTER EIGHT

I Get a Kick Out of You

"Sports do not build character. They reveal it."

—HEYWOOD HALE BROUN

Roughly 120 million individuals play soccer worldwide; 16 million play in the United States with half the players 5 to 14 years of age. Soccer is the fastest growing team sport in the United States. The success of our Olympic and Women's World Cup Champions only increased interest in the sport, an interest that is predicted to continue to grow in the coming decades.

Not surprisingly, soccer injuries have increased significantly as well. In the United States alone, over 220,000 individuals will seek emergency room attention for soccer related injuries this year according to the National Injury Electronic Surveillance System—a branch of the federal government. About 20% of these injuries are serious, necessitating admission to the hospital, surgery, or long-term care. Some 70% of soccer injuries occur in the lower extremities and 15% are injuries to the head. This figure actually underestimates head injuries because the vast majority are stealth injuries that go unreported. As cumulative injuries rather than acute injuries, they don't often result in emergency room visits and therefore aren't well documented.

I first began to see signs of soccer's increased popularity in the early 1990s; that's when an increasing number of kids with significant soccer related injuries began to come through the doors of our clinic. One incident attracted significant attention in our community; a child playing the goalie position sustained femur (thighbone) fractures in both of his legs and a severe concussion when two of his friends tipped the goal over on him. The femur fractures took roughly three months to heal, but the head injury had a more lasting affect—the child sustained permanent short-term memory loss. An A-B student prior to his injury, afterward the child became a C-D student.

Another child playing goalie in our community broke her neck when the wind blew the goal over on her. Fortunately for her, she didn't suffer long-term paralysis or muscle weakness, but she did need a halo device after her cervical fusion to stabilize her spine and prevent long-term problems.

After these two incidents, we searched the medical literature and found that over a 13-year time period, 18 children age 5 to 14 had died following soccer goalpost impacts. In fact, we found goalpost impact to be the most common cause of fatal injuries in soccer. These impact injuries included collisions with the goalpost, the wind blowing a goalpost over on a child, and someone tipping a goalpost over on a child. In some cases, children climbing on top of the goalpost had it fall on them, crush their chest, and kill them.

Soon after the two injuries in Ann Arbor, several other soccer goalpost injuries occurred in the U.S. This rash of injuries prompted the federal government to recommend that all fields in the United States equipped with soccer goalposts have them fixed to the field surface. Proponents of this measure hoped that it would prevent fatalities from tip-over injuries. The idea had some merit. But as we had seen in our study of softball sliding injuries, if you place a fixed immovable object on the field, individuals can and will collide with it and possibly injure themselves. In our community alone we saw several cases where kids collided with goalposts while running and chasing the ball. Many sustained serious head, neck, and extremity injuries.

So we decided to investigate these injuries at the Institute laboratory. We planned to conduct a series of tests looking at different types of padding materials that might reduce the force of impact. We decided to speak with several protective padding industry representatives about the project and ask if we could procure materials for testing. Bob Hensinger, a member of our Board, called me and said that he knew a gifted scientist with an engineering background who could contribute to our efforts at the Institute. He said his name was John Marcello and I should call him. A principal of the protective padding manufacturer Danmar Products, John had a long track record at developing padding systems for athletes. Soon after the call, I met him and found him to be incredibly enthusiastic and intelligent. Tall, slender, soft-spoken, and very analytical, John didn't fit the image of a former University of Michigan wrestler. But it was this athletic experience that led him to develop a special interest in designing wrestling helmets and helmet gear for motorcyclists and for handicapped children. This grew into an interest in developing other protective headgear, helmet structures, and padding. It was a natural alliance, and John has worked with us over the years in our testing of new materials.

I told John that we hoped to develop a thin padding system that would not alter the goal dimensions or appreciably alter the rebound of the ball, but still protect the child from impact with the post. We learned from our previous experience with breakaway bases that we couldn't use materials that interfered with the game as it is played. We knew, for example, that if we used large, thick padding that altered the goal dimensions, soccer officials would not agree to apply the material to goalposts. Furthermore, if the material significantly dampened the rebound of the ball, this could well alter the flow of the game, and soccer traditionalists would immediately reject the padding.

With John's help, we tested various types of composites. After two years of investigation, we found a material that would reduce the force of impact over 60%. It was like reducing the impact of hitting a brick wall to the impact of hitting a padded wall. Furthermore, the composite was thin and did not significantly alter the goal dimensions and did not appreciably alter the rebound of the ball.

So we conducted our testing in two different ways. First, we conducted a vertical drop test where we dropped a computerized head model on goalposts fitted with different types of padding. When we found a padding that led to a significant reduction in force, we moved on to a horizontal test. We used a mini crash sled with a computerized head and neck model and accelerated it down a track until it hit a goalpost fitted with different types of padding. After a series of laboratory tests, we found a material that was effective. We then decided to test it on soccer fields in Ann Arbor. We placed the padding on six fields in Ann Arbor and monitored play for a two-year time period. During that time, kids collided with the posts on 14 occasions. None sustained an injury, as opposed to our previous experiences with unpadded posts. No player, coach, referee, or spectator complained that the materials altered the rebound of the ball to any significant degree. Furthermore, the padding was thin enough to allow the goalpost to fall well within the rules for goal dimensions.

Avulsion injuries are another common occurrence involving soccer posts. Soccer nets often are hooked into the post and players can get caught on these hooks. On one occasion, we had a player in Ann Arbor who jumped up to get the ball and caught his ring on the hook. When he came down, his ring and finger remained on the hook. Such ring avulsion injuries are very severe and occur not infrequently internationally. The padding system we used snapped on rather than hooked on over the post and essentially eliminated the hook issue. So the padding system led to a reduction in force and eliminated avulsion injuries at the same time.

While conducting our soccer goalpost study, we discovered another problem occurring in the sport. While observing the games, we noticed that during practice, coaches in the youth leagues brought players over to the sideline and had them perform heading drills (heading is a technique used in soccer to advance a ball down the field by hitting it with one's head).

A coach would line children up in a long line and bounce the soccer ball off a child's head 10 or 15 times. The child would stagger away, then the coach would go to the next child and do the same thing. He would continue down the line until all the children were out on the field staggering around like little punch-drunk boxers.

When the children came off the field, I asked them, "What do you like best about soccer?" and received a myriad of responses. Then I asked, "What do you like least?" The kids answered uniformly, "Well, you know, that heading drill we did? When we're done heading the ball, I sometimes have blurred vision or double vision or ringing in the ears or bad headaches." Sometimes kids said they felt like they were going to "throw up." These are all common signs of concussions, and we well know from studies conducted in football and boxing, that these repetitive concussive events could become cumulative and lead to significant problems including loss of memory and cognitive functioning. I think all of us recall the picture of Muhammad Ali during the 1996 Olympics in Atlanta carrying the Olympic torch with a significant tremor and shaking. Such Parkinson-like syndromes can develop after multiple head impacts.

So we searched the internet for research on this problem. We found that researchers recently had presented a study on heading in soccer at a conference in Oslo, Norway. The researchers followed a group of soccer athletes 19 years of age and greater, and found that 81% developed permanent information processing deficits and memory loss solely related to heading. Some members of the soccer community expressed concern about the results of this study, while traditionalists dismissed the study because it pointed out a problem within the sport.

Clinical researchers involved in injury prevention are not doomsayers or naysayers; we want to develop safer sports practices so more individuals can participate in them for a longer period of time. As an orthopedic surgeon, I can tell you the major reason individuals quit a sport is injury. If we can find a way to prevent injuries in sports, we will have more individuals enjoying sports for a longer period of time. Many people think sports injuries are short-term events and don't have long-term ramifications, but in fact, when you're injured, it has an adverse affect on your work life and home life as well. Unfortunately, many traditionalists in the sport, whether it's soccer, baseball, softball, hockey, or football, feel that any attention drawn to injuries will demean the sport and prevent children and adults from participating. This couldn't be further from the truth.

So we went to the soccer community in Ann Arbor and related our findings, the findings in the study from Europe, and our findings from our interviews with kids after they had performed heading drills. It took us well over six months to speak to soccer officials, coaches, parents, and players' groups to get approval at all levels and to get all the paperwork signed so we could begin the study. However, once we began the study, the community proved to be very supportive. Several individuals played a significant role in the study: Angela Cheney, Cindy Bir, Beth Kedroske, and my old college roommate, Dr. Rich Salamone. With his background in neuropsychology he helped develop a neuropsychological testing program for student athletes in Ann Arbor on information processing and memory deficits due to heading. I asked him to find an effective program that we could modify for our study. He found a testing protocol used in other studies and made some modifications. The protocol consisted of verbal testing and written testing of information processing and memory abilities.

We recruited several coaches and assistant coaches and, with funding assistance from the McDonald's Corporation, instituted a study where we followed 57 students, boys and girls ages 11–14, over a two-year period of time, We followed the athletes through spring, summer, and fall seasons and tested their cognitive abilities before the beginning of each season and at the end of each season. Then we interviewed each child about concussive symptoms they developed including episodes of blurred vision, double vision, nausea, vomiting, ringing in the ears, and headache. Field supervisors, parents, and coaches recorded heading events for each child at each practice, as well as during each game.

At the end of the first set of seasons—three seasons occur annually in Ann Arbor—spring, summer and fall—we found that over 49% of the players developed recurrent concussive symptoms, most commonly headaches. These symptoms lasted long after practice and long after games and appeared related to episodes of heading rather than collisions.

We also did neuropsychological testing on the athletes both before and after the season. At the end of the first season, we found no statistically significant difference in information processing and memory ability compared to athletes in a standardized control group. After the conclusion of a second year of testing, we found again that roughly 49% of players complained of concussive symptoms long after practices and games were over. And again, these symptoms appeared related to heading rather than collisions. We also found evidence that the players' information processing and memory testing abilities had begun to diminish to a small degree . We concluded while these deficits could not be considered permanent, continued exposure to heading with recurrent concussive events could well lead to permanent deficits such as those described in the Oslo study.

We took our findings to the Ann Arbor soccer community, including parents, coaches, and officials. They asked us, "Should we put helmets on all the kids?" After our experience with softer baseballs and chest-protectors for baseball, we didn't want to place our hopes and good wishes ahead of testing and science. Although intuitively helmets might work, they possibly could be more harmful than helpful. So before we made any recommendations on helmet use, we conducted some research on some primitive helmet prototypes that potentially could be used. John Marcello and Danmar Products developed some early-stage prototypes for us to test. Based on our findings, we recommended that a helmet structure include the following: (1) it should reduce the force of impact significantly; (2) it should dissipate heat so that children would not become overheated and possibly victims of heat exhaustion; and, (3) it should be physically appealing to children. Kids want a helmet that lets them look like Darth Vader and not a nerd. We contacted several helmet manufacturers and suggested that they create such a helmet, but to date we know of no prototype that meets all three criteria. Danmar and John Marcello continue to work to this day attempting to incorporate these three elements into a helmet.

Some of the soccer coaches in our community suggested that perhaps during the soccer drills, we could let a little of the air out of the ball. They felt this might protect the kids. We considered this suggestion, but found we ran into the same problem that we had with softer baseballs, i.e., that when we let the air out of the ball, it actually stuck to the child's head for a longer period of time upon impact, and potentially delivered more of a blow with more force and momentum to the child's head. Thus this measure could potentially increase rather than diminish the risk of injury. We suggested that instead of letting air out of the ball, teams could use a lightweight beach ball the size of a soccer ball during heading drills.

Of course, the ultimate solution would be to abolish heading, but soccer officials, players, coaches, and parents objected to this, since heading is such an integral part of the game. Getting teams to comply with this measure is rather like getting softball teams to abolish sliding. Short of abolishing heading, using a lightweight, beach ball-like soccer ball during drills could eliminate most of the risk. Beyond this, instruction in proper heading technique is essential. Hopefully, sporting goods manufacturers will develop prototypes that we can test in the future that will reduce the force of impact significantly and meet the other criteria we outlined.

About this time, we began to see another common soccer injury in our clinic. Recreational soccer players began to show up in our clinic with broken shinbones (tibia), still wearing the shin guards they had put on to prevent these injuries. We began to ask ourselves what studies had been done on shin guards?

Soccer leagues internationally had mandated the use of shin guards and yet these injuries continued to occur. We did a literature search and found researchers in Germany had conducted a small study some years before with no conclusive findings. No further research had been conducted on this problem since that time. So we enlisted the help of Cindy Bir and Steve Cassatta, both mechanical engineers, in designing a study. Our friends and colleagues at the General Motors Research Labs donated a crash model leg to our laboratory on the campus of St. Joseph's Mercy Hospital for us to conduct impact testing. We positioned the crash dummy leg on a synthetic turf and had a weight on a pendulum impact the shin at a particular area with and without shin guards. Then we measured the force at this impact site and various levels up and down the leg.

Our studies showed that wearing any shin guard provided more protection than wearing no shin guard; however, the effectiveness of shin guards varied considerably. Air system shin guards proved more effective than shin guards with padding and plastic. Air systems distributed the impact in an east/west direction rather than in a north/south direction, reducing the force of impact up to 77%. In effect, it reduced the force from hitting a brick wall into the force of hitting a large feather pillow. The shin guard air systems use the bubble material that you find in packing and that most kids (and their parents) like to pop.

As I mentioned, soccer leagues worldwide mandated shin guards prior to our performing this study. We found that they mandated soccer shin guards following an incident that occurred in Europe. An HIV-positive player sustained a shin bone fracture and the bone penetrated the skin. The trainer who took care of the injury cut his hand on the exposed bone and contracted the AIDS virus. Soccer officials suggested shin guards might prevent AIDs. So practicing "safe soccer" with the use of shin guards can prevent many untoward consequences, but the greatest benefit is preventing shinbone fractures and contusions or bleeding around the bone.

I found the experience working with soccer communities to be very positive. We experienced little of the resistance we had in our other prevention studies and found parents, coaches, and officials to be highly involved in our studies. Among those involved, Steve Olsen, a member of our Advisory Board who helped run the intramural department at the University of Michigan, proved especially helpful. A great analyst of the sport, he can break down the rules, techniques, and other components of soccer in a fashion I've never seen anyone do before. He's extremely open-minded and has only one interest at heart, the health and welfare of the players. Traditionalism takes a backseat. One of the leading soccer officials in the United States, Steve has refereed at the World Cup level. He gave us great insight into soccer rules and procedures and helped us develop a national network of soccer officials, coaches, and soccer reporters with whom we could discuss our findings and integrate our research.

Soccer officials proved interested in our suggestions and, in fact, acted on these suggestions without hesitation and in a very timely fashion. I must say, this is in marked contrast to our experience with the softball and baseball communities on a national level. Why would two sports communities be so different in their response to prevention issues? I think it's probably because soccer is a relatively new sport in the United States and doesn't have the ingrained traditions found among more established soccer communities in Europe or South America. I believe American soccer enthusiasts are somewhat more open-minded and interested in any measures that might lead to more appeal for the sport in the U.S. Clearly members of the soccer community embraced the philosophy that if we prevent injuries, more people will participate in the sports for a longer time. In contrast, officials at all levels of baseball, including recreational, amateur, semipro and pro level officials, expressed the attitude, "Why should we care about injuries? If people don't know the proper technique and get hurt, it's their own fault." It's a Darwinian "survival of the fittest" philosophy that I feel has no place in sports, particularly in children's sports.

Many people ask me about our two children and whether we encourage them to play sports. Our girls, Allison and Katie, participate in sports and are quite good golfers. They also play in the local soccer leagues. I believe each sport has potential risks and possible injury associated with the particular sport, but we find that we can attenuate many of those risks through appropriate training, coaching, conditioning, and teaching the fundamentals of the sport. When it comes to heading, our girls know that Dad doesn't really think that it's a good thing to do, and they have found within the rules various techniques of knocking the ball down and advancing it down the field without heading. I must say that their teams don't seem to lack in competitiveness despite the fact that they don't head, and they've thoroughly enjoyed the sport of soccer.

I would highly recommend the sport to any parent or student athlete. It's a great aerobic activity and teaches great sportsmanship and team camaraderie. As with any sport, one of the most valuable lessons you receive is learning how to lose. I don't believe in Vince Lombardi's "winning is everything" and "winning is the only thing" philosophy. We all like to be winners and it's easy to be a winner. It's harder to be a gracious winner, but the most valuable lesson I ever received from sports and in watching my children play soccer, is actually learning how to be good losers. Soccer, as with any sport, is a microcosm of life. You cannot win at every aspect. You can try. You can give it 110%, but sometimes, probably most of the time, you are not going to be Number One. You need to assess why you didn't win and go back to the drawing board so that you can become a better player or a better person down life's road. To quote Emerson, "Bad times have a scientific value. These are occasions a good learner would not miss." I would add to Mr. Emerson's passage ". . . a good learner and athlete would not miss."

CHAPTER NINE

An Ambassador of Prevention

"Travel is fatal to prejudice, bigotry, and narrow-mindedness, and many of our people need it sorely on these accounts. Broad, wholesome, charitable views of men and things cannot be acquired by vegetating in one little corner of the earth all one's lifetime."

—MARK TWAIN, *INNOCENTS ABROAD*, 1869

Over the years I've had the opportunity and privilege to speak about prevention and health care cost containment before several hundred organizations. These organizations have ranged from Brownie and Girl Scout troops to international distinguished groups of physicians, nurses, and health care providers with audiences from ten to several hundred. Over the years, many people have asked me why I take the time and effort to give these presentations, particularly the talks to small groups. If I can convince one or two people in the audience about the paramount importance of prevention, they will go back to their communities and literally impact thousands of individuals participating in sports from the youth to the senior level.

The key message I try to convey in my presentations is that a small outlay in time, effort, and money in prevention can have enormous positive ramifications. Preventative efforts can lead to significant reductions in disability and health care expenditures. I always comment that no one will ever come up to you and thank you for preventing his/her injury. More than likely, he/she will have no knowledge of your efforts which is fine—that isn't what's important. I measure my success by a reduction in the number of injuries I see in my clinic. For every soccer, softball, or football game that is played without an injury, that is a success for every parent, teacher, coach, and community.

Injury is a national and international unrecognized public health problem that transcends age, race, gender, and state and national borders. I have found ambassadors of prevention at every level.

Local groups are my favorite to address; I've had an opportunity to present to Rotary Clubs, Boosters Groups, and other community groups throughout the country. I love the interaction that small groups present. When I have the opportunity to discuss prevention one on one, they understand the impact injury has on their friends, family, and community and the importance of injury prevention. It then becomes a quick transformation to an injury prevention ambassador. I have found that at the local level, people integrate the changes that we have proposed in the most expeditious manner. Giving lectures at the national level can also prove extremely important; however, the closer one can get to local communities, the more impact you will have in the long run.

In fact, several surgeons in Raleigh, NC approached me after one of my presentations about where they could purchase the breakaway bases for their communities. It was a great feeling to get such a positive, immediate response.

We have built many bridges over the years with leading

national organizations within the field of orthopedics. I've had the opportunity of presenting at the American Academy of Orthopedic Surgeons annual meeting on several occasions, as well as at several events hosted by the American Orthopedic Foot and Ankle Society. I must say, the Foot and Ankle Society was the first organization in orthopedics to recognize the importance of prevention and prevention-related research.

We also have received one of the highest honors bestowed in the sports medicine community, the American Orthopedic Society for Sports Medicine Award for Best Clinical Research in North America. We received this distinction for our research on breakaway bases. Receiving this honor, as well as having the opportunity to present our research to the AOSSM membership proved a great privilege and hopefully led some leading sports medicine physicians to take preventative measures back to their communities.

Two very memorable trips to New York City occurred several years apart. The first happened when the American Orthopedic Foot and Ankle Society (AOFAS) recognized the Institute and our research on preventing needless foot and ankle injuries through the use of breakaway bases. The leadership of the Society adopted a position statement recommending the use of breakaway bases on recreational fields throughout the country. The Society scheduled a news conference in New York City to announce the position statement and bring our findings to the attention of the general public. All of us at the Institute were thrilled by the Society's action, and I was particularly thrilled to be asked by this, the most prestigious group of foot and ankle surgeons in North America, to speak on behalf of the Institute and present our research to the national media at the press conference. Alas, it was not to be. Just two weeks prior to the event, my daughter, Allison, contracted chicken pox. Now normally a child developing chicken pox is not a major or at least not an uncommon event in a family's life; however, because of Allison's significant viral infection at the ripe old age of 11 months, we felt very concerned. Chicken pox also is a significant viral illness and we weren't sure how much her immune system had recovered. Some kids develop a type of pneumonia with chicken pox and can become gravely ill. So we battled through the chicken pox with Allison and she successfully turned aside the virus. Unfortunately, our two-year old daughter Katie developed the chicken pox in turn and promptly passed it on to her dad.

When I called Rich Cantrall, the American Orthopedic Foot and Ankle Society Executive Director, to give him the news, I think he thought I was kidding. I told him I had been exposed to chickenpox and didn't think I could come to New York. And, sure enough, two days before the event I broke out in a rash, developed chills and fevers, and had a rip-roaring case of chicken pox. It was too late to reschedule the event. So we had to improvise.

With the help of Rich Cantrall and Andy Walker, an attorney friend of mine who planned to visit New York at the time, we ended up pulling off the press conference. Andy brought my slides to New York and Rich set them up while I gave my presentation over a speakerphone, prompting Andy as to when to advance the slides. At the conclusion of the half-hour presentation, I took questions from the press over the phone, and the event actually received excellent coverage. In fact, the presentation probably went better than if I had been there in person. Rich has been an extremely important person in the presentation of our prevention research, and is truly responsible for pushing the prevention ball down the field to a significant degree. Without an ambassador like Rich, we would not have received the attention we have over the years.

A few years later, again in New York, I was invited by the American Academy of Orthopedic Surgeons (AAOS) to speak at their Science Writer Seminar in New York. Every year the Academy hosts the one-day event to outline developments within the field of orthopedics and sports medicine that could well lead to a safer and healthier America. The Academy really has been on the forefront of prevention within the medical field. Several hundred individuals from the electronic and print media are invited to hear about eight to ten presentations throughout the day during this event.

I arrived in New York City on a sunny October afternoon in 1997. The event was to be held at the Grand Hyatt near Grand Central Station in Manhattan. I hopped in a cab at Kennedy Airport and asked the cab driver to drop me off at the hotel, then wait while I dropped off my bags. I left them at the desk, rushed back to the cab, jumped in and asked the cabby to drive me down to Wall Street so I could take a look around. He obliged and we headed down Broadway. As we approached Wall Street, the cabby sensed that something was wrong. "There are too many people outside at this time of day," he said. This was about 2:30 p.m. I got out of the cab and paid my fare. I turned around and stood before a four-story stone building. Two men, probably in their thirties, stood there with their heads buried in their hands. "What's wrong?" I asked one of them.

"The market's crashed and it's an absolute disaster," he responded.

I turned and saw another gentleman, probably in his early sixties, who stood there calmly surveying the scene. I said to him, "These guys seem pretty upset. How come you're not?"

"This is the first bear market that these guys have ever seen," he told me. "I've been through so many of them, it just doesn't get to me anymore." He informed me that the downside hadn't arrived. The market was just closed for about a half-hour until it could reopen. This was just after Wall Street introduced "curbs." When the market reaches a certain level, it automatically closes for 30 minutes. Curbs were designed to reduce the risk of panic and a further downturn. "I bet you we go down another couple hundred points and it'll close again for the day," the older gentleman said. Then he asked me, "Why don't you stick around for awhile and we'll talk afterward to see if I was right." Well, sure enough, he went in around 3 p.m. and not later than 3:10 or 3:15 p.m. returned with the news that the market had plummeted another 200 points and that they were done for the day.

"How much further is this going to go?" I asked him. He looked up at the skyscrapers surrounding us and said, " I see no one on the ledges, so there's still some downside left." This somewhat morose statement was undoubtedly true. He informed me that markets don't go straight up, and can go down significantly at times, but they always come back. He asked me, " What did you do in '87?" I responded that in '87 I didn't have much money to play the stock market, so essentially, I didn't do anything. "Well," he said. "If you don't do anything this time, you'll do just as well as you did back then just holding on. In fact, if you have a little extra money, wait until tomorrow morning after 11 a.m., and then buy in and you'll find that things will start moving up again."

I asked him how he knew this and he informed me that he had been watching how money had been flowing in and out of the market and who was putting money in and out in the big transactions. He felt that this was a short-term event and that the market would bounce back much more quickly than it did in 1987. Well, I wish I knew who that fellow was because the next day around 11 or 11:30 a.m., the market started to bounce back. I have never had the opportunity to thank the person who gave me the best financial advice of my life and a very valuable lesson on Wall Street that day.

The next day I spoke at the science writer's seminar and you could feel the tension in the air; people were concerned about the stock market and potential economic downturn. It seemed each reporter was on their cellular phone every 5 minutes over the latest market gyration. Nevertheless, the presentation was successful and led to a series of feature articles on health care prevention in magazines and newspapers throughout North America. I was pleased with the response; rarely do you have the opportunity to give a presentation and deliver a message that reaches the public at large so quickly.

We also have had success in delivering our message of injury prevention and health care cost containment to the international community as well. Canada has embraced our research and preventative message most strongly. The Canadians have significant experience with hockey injuries and Canada is the home to much of the research on preventing these injuries. I have had the opportunity of presenting in London, Toronto, Banff, Vancouver and Ottawa. My visits to Canada have introduced me to many organizations and many people who have become tremendous friends and provided great support for our work. In particular, the Canadian Academy of Sport Medicine has stepped to the plate.

The Institute and I were fortunate to receive the R. Tait McKenzie Award at the International Congress and Exposition on Sports Medicine and Human Performance in Vancouver hosted by the Canadian Academy. The R. Tait McKenzie Award is given to individuals and organizations for significant contributions in the field of sports medicine, and in particular, contributions in the area of prevention and clinical research. It is one of the highest honors that the Institute and I ever received, and I truly cherish it.

I also represented the Institute as the Tom Pashby Lecturer at a meeting hosted by the Ontario Medical Association in Toronto. The Tom Pashby Award is given to innovators in sports injury prevention and is the highest honor that I've received. In fact, to be linked with Tom Pashby in any way is the highest honor. An ophthalmologist and caring and dedicated physician, Tom brought attention to the issue of blinding eye injuries within the sports of hockey, racquetball, and handball. He developed the face shield currently used in hockey, as well as the goalie mask and protective eyewear for racket sports. His efforts have prevented millions of eye injuries, including tens of thousands of blinding eye injuries, and saved millions of dollars in health care expenditures. Tom's dedication truly serves as an inspiration to every clinical researcher. All of us strive to have the public service impact he has manifested throughout his career, although we know none of us will ever reach the heights that Tom has attained.

As I previously mentioned, I had the opportunity to complete a sports medicine fellowship (focusing on shoulder reconstruction surgery) under the direction of Dr. Rich Hawkins at the University of Western Ontario in London, Ontario, Canada. I also had the opportunity to work with Dr. Peter Fowler, director of sports medicine at the same institution and one of the leading knee reconstruction surgeons in the world. An outstanding individual who truly loves life, Pete likewise is loved by many.

Pete and Hawk proved instrumental in the implementation of the breakaway bases in our professional baseball study as well as throughout Canada. Pete invited me to be the keynote lecturer at the University of Western Ontario Sports Medicine Annual Symposium. Over the years, Pete has brought our research efforts to the National Alliance for Safer Sport. Based at the University of Western Ontario, the alliance focuses on prevention and public education on sports injuries throughout Canada.

The American Orthopedic Foot and Ankle Society has several members in Canada. In fact, they held one of their national conferences in Banff, Alberta, undoubtedly one of the most beautiful places on the face of the earth. Pristine and lush beyond belief, Banff is situated in the Canadian Rockies where towering peaks and jagged cliffs rise above incredibly clear turquoise lakes. My parents, my wife, and our two girls accompanied me on this trip. During my childhood, my parents and I vacationed in Banff several times. Banff and Alberta have changed significantly since that time. Once a small resort town, Banff now has become an international tourist attraction and Japanese tourists, in particular, frequent the area. In fact, Banff and the surrounding area feature prominently in a Japanese soap opera.

The most popular Janda with the Japanese was then-four-year-old, red-haired, blue-eyed Allison. Groups of Japanese people would surround her and shower her with candy in the hope that they could get a picture with her. Apparently, individuals with red hair and blue eyes in Japan are extremely rare, and folks went crazy over her. We'd walk through the hotel lobby, and the Japanese guests would turn around and clap for her. She would just stand there and people would rush up to her and ask to hold her and take pictures. Being a smart little girl, Allison soon learned to take advantage of this attention. She would just say, "Candy?" And sure enough someone would thrust candy her way in very short order.

During my keynote address, Allison and my wife Libby sat in the back of the room. Allison used the occasion to tell her little joke that started when she was very, very young; roughly six months of age. I started to speak and she hollered out, "Mamma!" I began to laugh at this, our inside joke. Her mom didn't find the situation so humorous. Immediately, Libby whisked Allison away so Dad could continue his presentation.

Later that day, we drove by the Banff Springs Golf Course on the way to lunch. As we passed the course, I happened to glance over toward a shed, actually an outhouse, and saw a group of golfers running toward it. Close on their heels were several very large elk. Apparently, the golfers had driven their golf balls into the elks' territory. The elk didn't take kindly to this intrusion and proceeded to stampede the golfers. Now, I've had an opportunity to review the literature on golfing injuries. In fact, I had an opportunity to do some work with *Golf Digest* magazine on golf-related injuries; specifically, they ran a story about tests we conducted on head impact injuries from golf balls and golf clubs (approximately 40,000 golfers are admitted to emergency rooms each year from golf injuries). But I must say that nothing prepared me for the sight of these elk chasing four grown men into an outhouse.

Having these men barricade themselves in the bathroom while the elk lowered their antlers and battered it proved a surreal experience. However, this appears to be a fairly common occurrence in Banff; after five minutes of this barrage, the park rangers nonchalantly strolled by and freed the four golfers from their outhouse imprisonment.

One of my favorite trips to Canada occurred when I visited the capital city, Ottawa, to speak at the Canadian Academy of Sport Medicine Annual Meeting. My good friend and orthopedic group colleague, Dr. Derek Mackesy, also presented. A family practice physician who specializes in the care of injured athletes and has earned the respect of the NHL players and coaches alike, he has earned this respect from not only taking care of them when injured but also counseling them on prevention techniques to enhance and prolong their careers. They truly know he is on their side. This was evident when I saw firsthand, their devotion to him in Ottawa.

In Ottawa we stayed at Chateau Laurier, a beautiful, gothic style stone-built hotel near Ottawa's Capitol Hill. It was a bitterly cold February day. Derek had mentioned that after dinner he planned to attend the Ottawa Senators' hockey game against the Tampa Bay Lightning. He asked me if I wanted to go, and I said sure. We took a taxi to the arena, which was built beneath the football stadium at one end of the football field underneath the cement grandstands. As we got out of the cab, I asked Derek, "Where are the tickets?" He told me he didn't have them.

"We'll just go in here," he said as he led me to the players' entrance. An elderly man greeted him like a long-lost brother, giving him a big bear hug and welcoming him to the city of Ottawa and the home of the Ottawa Senators. He then whisked us outside the team locker room. Terry Crisp, the coach of the Tampa Bay Lightning, stood in the hallway doing an interview with TV commentators. He saw Derek and said, "Let's hold on the interview for a sec." The interview halted and he walked over to Derek and gave him a bear hug. Then Rich Bonnass, the coach of the Ottawa Senators, came out of the locker room and immediately went up to Derek and also gave him a big hug. Several players followed suit. In fact, I am convinced that Derek held up the game that night as all the players from both teams came over to greet him. We finished the greetings and went up to our seats. Not 15 minutes after we were seated, a tall, slender, mustached man in a sweater and tie came up behind Derek and tapped him on the shoulder. It was Roy MacGregor, one of Canada's most renowned authors and writers. The only person who didn't know Derek was the concession stand server, which was unfortunate since neither of us had any Canadian money in our pockets.

After the game, we went back down to the locker room. I found it truly a testament to Derek's popularity that players coming out of the locker room would come over and talk to him and me before moving on to the huge number of women onlookers and friends. We didn't take a taxi back to the hotel. Instead, the famous journalist and author MacGregor offered to give us a lift in his four-door late model sedan. I just didn't think that things could get much better than this. We spent the trip back to the

hotel discussing sports injury prevention and the trials and tribu-
lations of the Senators, who were on a major losing streak.

We got back to our hotel and went to our respective rooms. I
thought we had had enough excitement for the evening. But about
3 a.m., a fire alarm went off and we had to evacuate the hotel.
Derek and I stood outside in our pajamas and trench coats waiting for the all clear. It had to be 50 degrees below zero. It was just
horrid. So we began walking in downtown Ottawa just to stay
warm. All I could think about was that somehow we had become
some nightmarish version of the characters in the film *Thelma and
Louise*. Here we were walking down the streets of Ottawa in the
wee hours of the morning, looking like flashers in our pajamas and
trench coats.

As we walked back into the hotel lobby, some guy called out,
"Hey, Derek. What's going on?" It happened to be Mike Keenan,
the coach of the New York Rangers. He, too, was staying at the
Chateau Laurier, because the Rangers played Ottawa the next
evening. After the alarm ended, I headed back to my room, since
I had to give my presentation the next day. Derek went on with
Mike Keenan and ended up spending most of the night talking
with Mike and Mark Messier and several of the New York
Rangers. The final example of his place in injury prevention is that
Wayne Gretzky personally asked him to be the team physician for
the group of NHL All-Stars who went on a European exhibition
tour. Derek is an ambassador of how to implement prevention at
the highest level of sports.

Derek has been one of the most important role models in my
life. He exemplifies the well-rounded individual, good at his profession and dedicated to his family. And he's a heck of a nice guy
as well.

I also have presented our prevention research in Europe. The
most memorable occasion occurred when the French government

invited me to speak at the Cindyniecs Second International Colloquia in Paris at the Grand Amphitheater of the Sorbonne. The event brought together researchers and specialists in sports and other fields to discuss injury prevention. I had the opportunity to speak on the same panel as the famous oceanographer Jacques Cousteau. I wondered if I belonged—after all, this was Jacques Cousteau. A high official with the World Health Organization moderated the panel. (Cousteau spoke on the risk of ocean related injuries.) I found it truly an honor to speak at this event, and both Libby and I shared many wonderful moments with the participants and organizers.

The panel consisted of four presenters, each speaking for roughly one-half hour. About 15 minutes before our panel began, I noticed that the other three presenters appeared nervous. Some were trembling. I found this unusual because these individuals undoubtedly had presented hundreds of times before very large and very small groups and undoubtedly did so while maintaining a calm demeanor. Something seemed to be different about this event. Being a midwestern hick, I was clueless. I asked one of the presenters about this and he said it had to do with the history and grandeur of the Sorbornne. "There is no more prestigious place to present," he noted as he waved out toward this beautiful centuries-old, marble-floored auditorium with a huge 100-foot tall ceiling.

The place does evoke a sense of awe. You can sense the presence of Molière, Rodin, and Voltaire. In fact, huge statutes of them and six other outstanding French intellectuals stand in small alcoves built into the side of the auditorium. While I was observing this panorama, an official from the World Health Organization walked up to me. "Dr. Janda," he said. "You don't seem to be very nervous about presenting."

I answered, "Well, it's a topic that I've had the opportunity of addressing and working on for a long time."

"Don't the surroundings make you the least bit nervous?" he asked.

"Yes," I said. "It is a bit intimidating, such a prestigious facility with such a grand history behind it." He asked me if we had any facilities in America as grand. Before I could think, I blurted out "Yankee Stadium."

"Do they have statues like these in Yankee Stadium?" he asked.

"Well, yeah, kinda," I said. "They have statues of DiMaggio and Mantle and Gehrig and Ruth."

"These people you mentioned," he said, "are they American philosophers?"

"Well," I told him. "Yogi Berra is the only one in the group who was a philosopher."

Needless to say, I was kidding, but he didn't have much of a sense of humor about it and walked away shaking his head in disgust, not understanding nor willing to try. In all seriousness, if you ever visit Paris, go to the Sorbonne and the Grand Amphitheater. I truly found this to be one of the most magnificent facilities I've ever seen.

The Australians have also embraced our research and preventative efforts. Preventative health care is their model. The result has been a significant reduction of injuries and increased health care savings in Australia over the last decade. In fact, the Australians implemented many of the measures we have proposed during the 2000 Olympic games in Sydney, including breakaway bases and padded goalposts.

In 1996, the Australian Conference of Science and Medicine in Sports held its annual meeting in Canberra, the capitol of Australia. I was invited to address the conference. Many of the leading sports medicine officials and health care providers in Australia attend this conference. Under the direction of Donna Harvey, the conference coordinator, the event proved to be truly outstanding.

Well-organized and informative, it featured high quality presentations and a very enthusiastic, eager to learn audience. During this visit, I also presented our findings to a conference organized by Dr. Carolyn Finch, a public health official whose work focused on sports injury prevention, at Monash University in Melbourne.

I still keep in close touch with Donna Harvey, Carolyn Finch, and John Anderson, who ran the government's health insurance branch. A visionary in Australia and all of sports medicine, John has done what no other government official or insurance executive in the world has accomplished. He has made prevention a central focus of the insurance industry. If it seems natural that this would occur internationally, but I must tell you, that I know of no other organization in the world that links insurance with prevention, other than the New South Wales's government under the direction of John Anderson. This should be the rule but is truly the exception to the rule.

John invited my family and me back to Australia in November 1998, where he asked me to address the "Play it Safe" Conference hosted by the New South Wales government. I accepted his invitation and flew over to Sydney a year later. I gave two presentations at the conference. One talk focused on prevention within sport and I called it *Prevention Has Everything To Do with Sports Medicine*. The presentation went extremely well and several hundred physicians, nurses, physical therapists, and government officials from throughout Australia attended and brought the message back to their communities.

John also had asked me to lecture on the role of the legal community in prevention. As an attorney and one who knows my animosity toward the legal profession, my wife Libby cringed at the suggestion. "Thank God they're having you speak on this topic on another continent," she said. I began the presentation, on what I thought was a high note, quoting Shakespeare. I used the few words I could remember from my Shakespeare course at Bucknell University. An English major, Libby convinced me to take the Shakespeare course, which, as a chemistry and economics major, I found unbelievably boring. I told my audience that my presentation could be summed up in just one line from Shakespeare's Henry VI. "The first thing we do, let's kill all the lawyers."

Despite my rather feeble attempt at humor, the presentation went off well. My comments focused on how the legal community hampers preventative efforts by defending unethical business practices. I tempered my remarks by noting that some elements of the legal community, mainly my wife and her firm, have attacked businesses using unethical practices and defended those who undertook preventative efforts.

New South Wales played a prominent role in the 2000 Sydney Olympic Games and Justin Barwick, a government official in charge of the Olympics, gave us a tour of Sydney and Homebush, the site of the Olympics—at that point, just a hole in the ground. Only the aquatic center had been completed. Besides being a great diving facility, the aquatic center is a family recreation area complete with water slides; the Australians always try to mix business with pleasure. The girls and I decided to adopt the custom and did a couple of laps in the Olympic pool.

When John Anderson invited me to speak in Australia, he asked if I would also speak to community groups and school groups as well as appear on Australian TV and radio. I told John that I felt that speaking to small groups, and in particular, to school groups, has the largest positive impact on preventative efforts. Many lecturers don't want to address students; however, I believe if you can inspire one student at a conference to become involved with medicine, in particular, injury prevention issues and public health issues, you will multiply your efforts a thousandfold.

While visiting in Australia, John and I flew to Albury, a hot dusty city in the outback. I spoke there to school groups and community groups and conducted several TV and radio interviews. Albury was hot, but it got very hot very quickly once we left it and traveled through the outback and such towns as Tamworth, the country & western capitol of Australia. While there, I again spoke to school groups and community groups, and conducted TV and radio interviews. I must say Tamworth is no Nashville. It has a small country & western museum, but it's no Dollywood. But Tamworth has its own rugged outback style and its hardy residents were warm and gracious. And the local auditorium is one-fifth the size of the Grand Ole Opry. My favorite town in the outback, Wagga-Wagga, was so hot that you could fry an egg on the main street. The Aborigine words, wagga-wagga mean "many crows" and the town lived up to its name. Swarms of huge flies surrounded you everywhere you went in Wagga-Wagga. During an interview there, I had a difficult time keeping the flies out of my mouth. I thought it impolite to appear to be disturbed by them and kept talking as if nothing were going on. I must have swallowed a hundred of them. Later, I was told that it's considered proper and quite commonplace to wave flies away from your face during interviews. In fact, it's called the Aussie salute.

I finished presenting in Wagga-Wagga at approximately 9:00 at night and we drove on to Albury. The highway system in Australia, at least toward the outback, is rather different from any that I had previously experienced. You can drive on asphalt roads for hours without finding any remote semblance of human life, let alone a town. There's nothing but sand and tumbleweeds. Occasionally you see a "road train," two, three or even four 18-wheelers hitched together to save on gas. They're a major cause of highway fatalities in the outback and, if you see them, you get out of the way quickly.

While we were driving, John and his assistant must have wondered whether I had ever traveled outside of urban Michigan, because I kept sticking my head out the car window to stare up at the billions of stars before us. In rural communities through which I have traveled, you can see millions of stars in the sky, but this went far beyond those numbers. As I stared up, I saw some stars moving rapidly across the sky, and mentioned this to John. "Mate," he said. "Those are satellites going by." I found it amazing you could see satellites whizzing before you.

After a while, I grew tired of sticking my head out the window like our golden retriever Molly and turned my attention back to the road. I hadn't seen a gas station in a good two hours during our drive, and I asked John if he kept extra gas in the car. John mentioned that everyone took several articles with them when they drove at night in this part of the country, an extra can of gas and a gun.

"Now, why a gun?" I asked.

"Well," he said. "If you hit a kangaroo, which are plentiful in this part of the country, you just can't leave it to suffer. You have to shoot it."

I thought he was pulling my leg and said, "I don't see many kangaroos." John immediately turned off the paved two-lane road into the brush and flashed his lights. I looked out in astonishment at dozens of huge red kangaroos, each the size of a University of Michigan linebacker, bouncing in the outback. After a few minutes of this, John pulled back on the road. "Okay," I said. "So is that the only reason you keep a gun in the car?"

"Well no," he answered. "There's another reason. The wild boars." He proceeded to tell me that wild boars occasionally get turned on by car lights and will charge the car. They can actually disembowel a car and this has led to several fatalities on the highways. John told me that if you see one of these things coming at you, you need to hang your head outside the car, aim, and shoot before the boar hits you. Again, I thought that he was kidding, but when we got to Albury, I asked several people if this actually happened and they said it was commonplace.

We had wonderful experiences with our friends in Australia, and look forward to further visits in the years ahead as we try to integrate our injury prevention efforts with theirs.

When I look back at all my travels throughout the United States, Canada, Europe, and Australia, I find that my most cherished memories have been the relationships that I have developed and fostered. Whether it's speaking before the local Brownie troop, or a local community group, or before a national conference or international meeting in Canada, Europe, or Australia, it's the people I meet that provide the greatest pleasure. In all of these places, I've met people who realize the importance of preventive health care in their local and national communities and act on their awareness. The media also has played an important role in promulgating prevention. The people that seem to ignore the issue are the politicians, government officials, and many within the business community, particularly the insurance industry, and this also is true internationally. Others in corporate America talk the talk of prevention, yet when it comes time to walking the walk and supporting prevention efforts, they turn the other way. I would like to think that as time progresses, both the political elite and the business community will reach the level of awareness that can help prevent injuries internationally.

CHAPTER TEN

The Good, the Bad, and the Ugly

"Man is man because he is free to operate within the framework of his destiny. He is free to deliberate, to make decisions, and to choose between alternatives. He is distinguished from animals by his freedom to do evil or to do good and to walk the high road of beauty or tread the low road of ugly degeneracy."

—MARTIN LUTHER KING, JR.,
"THE MEASURES OF MAN," 1959

In my journey over the past decade and a half, I've experienced happiness, exhilaration, frustration, and utter anger and disappointment in my fellow human beings. I'm a little biased, but I believe, and many other individuals believe, the Institute has had an enormous impact on the sports population internationally. We're the only organization worldwide that focuses on sports injury prevention and its health care cost savings. Sports injury statistics worldwide are truly mind-boggling. In the United States alone, over four million children age five to fourteen will seek emergency room attention this year. Another eight million children will visit their primary-care physicians' offices for treatment of sports-related injuries. We contend that the vast majority of these injuries can be prevented.

You would think that no one would truly oppose the work of the Institute or any charitable organization that focuses on the prevention of youth and adult sports injuries. Unfortunately, such is not the case. Members of our board, advisory board, friends, and I face opposition on basically three fronts.

First we face opposition from those who doubt that the Institute genuinely has the interest of the public at heart. I can appreciate this concern. I welcome a healthy dose of cynicism in the sports medicine research arena where major economic interests are at play. Big money funds many medical studies and undermines their objectivity. For that reason, we structured the Institute to avoid potential conflicts of interest. We never have solicited, will never solicit, and have never received funding from sporting goods manufacturers. Some individuals seem to feel this decision suggests a snobbish attitude. We contend that to receive funding from sporting goods manufacturers or related corporations with a vested interest in our findings would truly compromise our research and represent a conflict of interest. Unfortunately some of this cynicism comes from individuals who let their egos get in the way of public health concerns. When one's professional expertise becomes more important than the public welfare, it tarnishes what researchers say and how they interact with our organization and other individuals within the medical community.

The second group of individuals I feel less generously inclined toward. These individuals oppose our efforts for economic reasons. As I noted above, many organizations and individuals make large sums of money selling sporting equipment products. We have no problem with companies earning a fair profit from sales of products; however we believe their sales and marketing efforts should be done in an honest and ethical manner. I believe that corporations and/or individuals should be held accountable for statements they make implying a public health benefit in their products. Slick marketing efforts and bought research shouldn't take the place of science. Our findings on their products have led to skirmishes, battles, and in several cases, all-out war with some sporting goods manufacturers. It's a war we can't lose. "It's all about science, and our data and our science are irrefutable," says one member of our advisory board. "What these other folks have is a bunch of trumped-up marketing, and in the long run they'll never win with their false claims." Even so, we're up against multimillion-dollar corporations that spend tens of thousands of dollars to discredit our work and it hasn't proved easy to do battle with them.

We always submit our research to the Institute's peer-review board. We also have submitted it to review by the General Motors peer review board and government agencies such as the CDC. Only after rigorous review by these boards will we submit our studies to peer-reviewed medical journals. Medical journal peer review boards thoroughly review and revise, and essentially dissect, our studies before they publish the results in the medical literature. Some individuals within health care tell me that peer review isn't necessary. But we believe it absolutely essential to the public welfare that scientific research be critically reviewed by unbiased observers and published by unbiased sources.

Finally, we face a more stealth type of opposition from the insurance industry. The insurance industry pays lip service to prevention, but refuses to support or endorse any prevention-related research. In fact, the insurance industry has given very little support to the concept of injury-prevention in sport, with the major exception of John Anderson and the New South Wales government in Australia. Insurance industry support would ensure the success of prevention-related efforts. Unfortunately, their silence on the matter has made the road much steeper and much harder to climb.

The Good

When I first proposed the founding of an Institute, several individuals stepped to the plate immediately. Some naysayers said that we would never develop a worthwhile board of directors. Fortunately, with the help of my colleagues at the Orthopedic Surgery Associates, we formed a board of directors internationally recognized as among the most innovative and progressive research boards. So we proved the naysayers wrong and pieced together a board of world-renowned physicians and medical specialists with an unparalleled track record in injury prevention. I find it amazing that not one of these individuals, since the Institute's inception, received pay to serve with it. All have donated their time and effort graciously and without a second thought. Our board remains the true core and nucleus of the Institute.

"So you got lucky forming a board of directors," said another group of naysayers. "You'll never be able to develop an advisory board worth anything. No famous athlete or business leader will ever donate time or effort to a fledgling non-university-based organization." We also proved those individuals wrong. It consists of former professional and Olympic athletes, business leaders, and individuals within communities who have made a significant difference to the public.

One of the first individuals to join the advisory board, Dr. David Viano, serves as the principal research scientist with General Motors. His work has taken the Institute to a higher plain, i.e., from a standard small clinic sports medicine approach to a high tech bioengineering approach. We spoke to many corporate executives about prevention, but few would accept our challenge to become involved. Dave joined after one phone call. I spoke with him about youth sports and chest impact injuries and fatalities, and immediately he said, "Sign us up. Let's try to find out what's happening and what we can do to alleviate this problem." Without the help and support of Dave and his colleagues at General Motors, Dick Thompson, Dennis Andreczak, and Joe McCleary, we never could have completed our first series of chest-impact studies. Without that first series of studies, advertising claims that softer baseballs and chest protectors prevent injury in youth sports would continue to mislead the public.

I thought that it might prove more than a little difficult to recruit former professional and athletes to the advisory board. I was wrong. I thought it would then be difficult to recruit Olympic athletes to our advisory board. I was wrong again. All proved more than willing to give their time and their effort to working with our organization because they understand better than most, because their bodies are so critical to their performance that they know the importance of injury prevention.

Initially, I thought that fund-raising would prove to be our easiest task. Boy, was I wrong. Even with our track record, outside funding has proven sparse, to say the least. Unfortunately, many corporate executives talk the talk of injury prevention, but few will actually fund studies or donate time or effort toward such issues. We hope others will join our business ambassadors including Dave Brandon, Chairman and CEO of Domino's Pizza; Bill Young, president of Absopure Water Company; Dave Sowerby, a chief analyst with Loomis-Sayles; and Bernie Banas of Hershey Foods. Without their support, we couldn't have advanced organizationally. Having business leaders committed to a research organization brings a different perspective—one to which few of us in medicine have been exposed.

Our plans to host a national symposium focusing on our

injury-prevention efforts brought forth another group of naysayers. They said we would never recruit enough registrants to make the conference work. We would lose a tremendous amount of money and the effort would prove an abysmal failure. Well, once again, we proved the naysayers wrong. With the help of Frank Svechota, Derrick Mackesy, Beth Kedroske, and Terri Jobkar, we developed one of the most prestigious international symposiums in sports medicine, the Mid-America Sports Medicine Symposium. Over the years, we have recruited a truly world-renowned faculty for the symposium. About 250 to 300 registrants attend annually. Our registrants include physicians, surgeons, nurses, therapists, athletic trainers, and biomechanical engineers from throughout the United States, Canada, Australia, South America, and Europe.

The symposium serves two purposes. The profit generated from the symposium helps support our injury prevention efforts. The symposium also generates more interest in injury prevention. When registrants leave the symposium, they return home armed with the latest preventative research and up-to-date treatment and prevention techniques. Furthermore, they become ambassadors for the Institute, bringing our prevention message home to their communities. Every year, we create 250 new ambassadors, and introduce 250 new communities to the benefits of injury prevention, including health care cost savings. Now in its eighth year, the symposium has introduced over 2,000 registrants to injury prevention—2,000 ambassadors who have returned to their communities and helped develop local prevention programs. So we proved wrong those who told us that we couldn't create a nationally—or internationally—known symposium. What's more, we've help foster a nurturing, educational environment for individuals and helped them bring prevention information to their own communities, thus extending the reach of the Institute by tens of thousands of miles.

Angela Cheney, Cindy Bir, and Beth Kedroske have served

on the front line for the Institute. Each of them has devoted many hours and much effort to our work on a day-to-day basis. I mentioned that the work of Dave Viano had catapulted us to a higher stage of development. The everyday involvement of Angela, Cindy, and Beth have contributed no less to the advancement of the Institute. Without their efforts, we would have made little impact over the past decade.

Countless individuals have stepped to the plate and helped us with our research, our symposium, and our auction. We created the auction in conjunction with the symposium to create more community awareness of our work in southeastern Michigan as well as to generate funds for our research. Dick Purtan, the leading morning show, radio disk-jockey in Detroit and Marconi Award Winner for U.S. Radio Personality of the Year, and Tim McCormick, former NBA standout and member of our advisory board, have taken the auction under their wings. They have transformed the event into one of our most successful fund-raising and public awareness efforts. Many others have helped with the auction, including Tara Beikman, Lisa Van Stone, Cathy Heller, Rhonda Papworth, Anne Judson, Bill and Denise Brandon, Karen Kohlman, Brenda Keiffer, Thais Lavaque, and Bev Penive, to name just a few. Without the effort of these individuals, the symposium, the auction, and much of our work could not have continued.

Over the years, dozens of TV and radio stories, and hundreds of newspaper and magazine articles have appeared on our work at the Institute. The media has played a significant role in the development of the Institute and in public awareness of what prevention can accomplish. We can conduct the best studies in the world and receive any number of national and international awards as well as significant notoriety within the medical community. But if the public does not become aware of our work, our efforts would prove absolutely fruitless. The media has taken our research and brought it to the public's door. Despite the common perception of the media as biased and sensationalizing, I have found most reporters to be extremely open, gracious, and generous as well as champions of injury prevention. Whether in Europe, Australia, the United States, or Canada, reporters demonstrate great interest in our studies and report our work in an honest and forthright manner 99% of the time. We at the Institute remain indebted to the members of the Fifth Estate for their continued attention to our studies and relentless pursuit of accurate health care information for the public.

After all the TV interviews I have done over the years, the program for which we received the most public response proved surprising to me. After I appeared on the "Today Show," the phone rang a fair amount, as it did with other network news shows. But the night the popular game show "Jeopardy" carried a question about our research and Alex Trebek mentioned one of our studies, the phone rang off the hook. Even my father called to tell me, "Kid, you've made it big! You were an answer on *Jeopardy*." I was shocked that my dad watched *Jeopardy*, let alone placed such importance on it.

The bottom line is that without the media's coverage of our work, our efforts at the Institute would lag far behind. Hundreds of print articles have appeared reporting on the work of the Institute, including articles in the *New York Times,* the *Washington Post,* the *Los Angeles Times,* the *Chicago Tribune, U.S.A. Today*, and the wire services. Usually folks want a copy of the study cited, which we gladly provide.

The Bad and the Ugly

As I mentioned earlier in this book, I believe that some organizations and individuals have unfairly represented the work of the Institute. In most cases, this misrepresentation appears to be driven by economic and financial concerns. Unfortunately the involved individuals have sufficient funds to compromise other organizations and provide misleading information to the public with pernicious consequences. The best that I can say about these individuals is, as Christopher Morley so aptly remarked in 1932, "A human being, an ingenious assembly of portable plumbing."

The benign neglect of the insurance industry provides another type of opposition that injury prevention researchers face. Interestingly, everywhere in the world injury prevention researchers say the same thing. The insurance industry has not stepped to the plate to develop or support injury prevention programs. The sole exception is the New South Wales government insurance plan. Unfortunately I could wallpaper the Taj Mahal and the Sistine chapel with the rejection letters we have received from insurance companies and insurance company foundations in response to our requests to support the Institute's work. The Institute has never received a dime's worth of funding for its prevention studies from the insurance industry—and not from a lack of trying on our part.

One night as my wife Libby and I watched "Larry King Live," an ad appeared for the AFLAC insurance company during a commercial break. The commercial has appeared many times nationwide. It features a baseball player running around bases. The player slides into third base late and hurts himself. He writhes around on the ground in obvious pain. Then the scene shifts to an insurance executive scratching his head as he looks at a form and says such things as, "Oh, the poor man" and "This would have been a good injury to prevent."

At that point, Libby turned to me and said, "Dave, that's your research. No one else has done this, and if they're using your research to support their insurance product, they should be interested in helping fund the Institute." So the next morning I forwarded a letter and information about the Institute to AFLAC, asking them to support our research. I soon received a reply from an AFLAC vice president stating that they don't support sports medicine research. Isn't it interesting that they use our research to advertise their product, but when asked to support it, they don't want to have a thing to do with the research. I never could quite figure out why the insurance industry would not support prevention research. It seems like a no-brainer. Prevention requires very little money up front. It can save a tremendous amount on health care costs that the insurance companies currently must pay.

I found the answer one day when I spoke with Jan Christenson, a member of the Governor's Council on Health, Fitness, and Sports in Michigan (I served on the Council with him). I told him that I could not figure out why the insurance industry wouldn't support our prevention efforts. He told me that he had similar experiences and then related a conversation he had with an old-time retired insurance industry executive. I later had a similar conversation with another insurance executive. It went something like this: "Son. The insurance industry not only won't support you, but they don't like what you do, and never will."

"Why is that?" I asked.

"Now, son! I know you're a doctor and doctors are terrible at money and finance, but maybe even you can figure this one out."

I listened intently.

"Son, if the cost of insuring you is $1,000, the insurance company can add 7% to that initial premium cost, and then your premium would be what?"

"Oh, $1070," I replied.

"Now, son," he said. "Let's say these insurance companies do everything you tell them to do, such as using breakaway bases, and they make the community safer. In fact, rates fall precipitously. Now the cost of insuring you is not $1,000, but $100. If they add the 7%, what's your premium?"

"$107," I respond.

"Now, Son, which would you rather have? Even you can figure this one out—seventy dollars or seven dollars?" So there is no incentive for insurance companies to save money because they pass on these costs directly to the consumer. Furthermore, they receive more premiums if the cost of insuring you is greater. State Insurance Commissions will give insurers their 7% no matter what the premium cost. Unfortunately, few in the insurance industry question this rationale. The insurance industry not only has failed to step to the plate to fund research to any significant degree, but to add insult to injury, most insurers do not give premium reductions to organizations that use sports protective equipment.

Some legal documents that came into my hands illustrate the problems we have had with sporting goods manufacturers. I do not testify in court cases, but rather encourage attorneys to use our published research as evidence in cases. If I wanted to, I could probably make a handsome living testifying in claims against manufacturers. I receive three to four calls a weeks asking me to serve as an expert witness in such claims. But my priorities are my patients and my research. However, on occasion, these requests do lead to some interesting documents coming into my hands. In October 1999, an attorney forwarded me a deposition with Mr. Jess Heald of the Worth Company, concerning the case of *Obyle vs. Little League Baseball* and dated August 26, 1996. As I mentioned earlier in the book, Mr. Heald is one of our fiercest adversaries on the injury prevention front. His company's advertising promotes softer, heavier baseballs and gives the impression they provide protection from injury and fatality. During Heald's testimony, he was asked, "Would it be fair to say that you don't know whether or not the softer baseball is more or less dangerous than the harder ball with chest impacts?" Mr. Heald answered under oath, "In terms of introducing a fatal heart arrhythmia, that's correct." In other words, under oath, he admitted that he doesn't know whether a softer baseball is in fact, less dangerous.

In an earlier 1992 deposition, Mr. Heald was asked whether he had devised any tests for chest-trauma injuries for softball and baseball, and he could only respond "No." If you review his statements to the press and the public, and if you look at his company's advertising, Heald implies and some times directly states a view 180 degrees opposite to his under oath testimony. When not under oath, he continues to tout the safety benefits of softer heavier baseballs.

Mr. Heald's stated opposition to our research is that it contradicts the research done by two individuals. Although they never published their research in the peer-reviewed medical literature, Mr. Heald and Worth promoted their studies as an alternative to the Institute's. In the documents presented to me in October of 1999, we found a letter to the researchers from Heald, signed "Jess" in which he states he is forwarding a check for $2,500 in half-payment for their paper on the "Critical Response to the GM Head-Impact Studies." Upon further examining these documents, it becomes clear that between April 1992, when our studies were about to be published, and 1994, the Worth Corporation, under Heald's signature, cut checks to one researcher and the institution where he was based for $46,400. In addition, Worth paid the other researcher and the institution where he was based $57,300 for the studies they completed for the Worth Corporation. And yet, Heald implies that they are independent researchers. Unfortunately their ruse has confused the public.

As I mentioned earlier, several corporations within the sporting goods industry suspect Mr. Heald, the Worth Corporation, and the relationship that they developed with the National Operating Committee for the Safety of Athletic Equipment (NOCSAE). I understand that NOCSAE terminated their relationship with their research director when it became evident that he had developed a financial relationship with the Worth Corporation. The true loser in this scenario of trumped-up research for financial gain is the public, who receives misleading information and poor advice.

Over the years, other organizations have attempted to step up to the plate, but faltered. In 1992, the American Academy of Pediatricians (AAP) issued a statement on baseball injury prevention. The statement was completely erroneous and actually stated that our research supported the use of magnetic bases. The only literature linking our study with magnetic bases was Riley-Meggs Industry's fraudulent advertising, over which we sued them. The AAP also linked our research and others' research to assertions that softer baseballs would prevent injuries—again truly erroneous information. After numerous calls to the AAP, I was told that a summer intern with little to no medical knowledge had written the document and the AAP released it to the press nationally. But the AAP does have a Sports Medicine Committee, which presumably would have reviewed the document. So I contacted the chairman of the AAP Sports Medicine Committee. He apologized but would do nothing. "Well, in three years we'll try to put out a press release that is more accurate," he told me. I find it absolutely astounding that a medical organization as prestigious as the American Academy of Pediatrics would distribute such an erroneous document, particularly one implying significant public health benefits, and, when the errors were pointed out, would do nothing to rescind their recommendations.

The battles continue and will continue, and we welcome individuals to question our research and to continue to research injury prevention on their own. No one at the Institute has ever said that we have all the answers. However, I do believe that comparing our studies to "bought" studies does a significant disservice to the public.

Our goal at the Institute is to provide high quality research that affects the public in a positive manner. We have found that you don't do anyone favors by telling them what they want to hear. We believe the true role of the Institute is telling people about what they need to know. We could have misrepresented our findings or not made our findings public and avoided an enormous amount of heat and pressure from multimillion dollar corporations. But our goal is to provide honest, scientific, independent research to the public and let the public decide what products they should or shouldn't use.

The individuals who have supported us from the beginning, the individuals who have doubted us from the beginning, and the individuals who have opposed us from the beginning all contributed to the development of the Institute. We hope to make our efforts on injury prevention worthy of those who support us. We further hope to make those who doubt our efforts ultimately come to the realization that they also should support our injury prevention efforts. And we hope to treat those who oppose our efforts fairly while working toward their defeat. These three groups of individuals, each in their own way, have taken the Institute to a higher level of development. Without the supporters, without the doubters, and without the opposition, we could not continue to thrive and prosper. Although we might not like the opposition, we have found that when we make our case to the general public, we create supporters out of doubters, and more fervent supporters out of our base supporters. And some times, the opposition actually become supporters, as well. The key to all of our work is perseverance, and never, never giving up. There are times when it seems that the battle might be over, but we always pursue it to the ultimate end. The formula for success is never taking no for an answer, and relentlessly pursuing the public interest.

CHAPTER ELEVEN

A Domestic Vietnam

"History is the torch that is meant to illuminate the past to guard us against the repetition of our mistakes of other days. We cannot join in the rewriting of history to make it conform to our comfort and convenience."

CLAUDE G. BOWERS

Becoming an orthopedic surgeon requires four years of medical school and five years of internship and residency. To make it through this grind takes several attributes. Chief among these is a relentless dedication to providing the best care. Many people believe it takes a bit of lunacy to give up some of the best years of your life cloistered in a room with medical books and working in isolation for unending hours with no one offering so much as a thank you. However, everyone who has gone through the training, the hardship, the financial costs, and the emotional costs of training, knows that after the first patient or the first patient's family thanks you for taking care of them or their loved one, all of your past effort seems worthwhile.

Unfortunately, the intrusion of government and the insurance industry into the health care field, has threatened the doctor/ patient relationship. These entities have attempted to coerce physicians into delivering less than quality care and into spending less time with patients. They also have limited the medicines physicians can prescribe, the types of treatment they can provide, the surgeries they can perform. Many good people have seen the writing on the wall and decided to use their talents in business and law rather than medicine. When we studied medicine, we were taught to deliver the highest quality of care possible. Insurance companies say "Forget all that. We will tell you how to care for your patients." We were taught to do no harm. Insurance companies say cut costs whether it harms patients or not. It's a war out there, a domestic Vietnam. Everyone sometime in life needs medical care and anyone who enters into the evolving health care system will be harmed to some degree. As grunts on the front line of this health care war, we physicians feel frustrated that government bureaucrats, business people, and insurance company executives with no functional medical knowledge make life and death decisions and continue to cast aside the most effective and humane approach to health care cost containment—prevention.

I've lectured throughout the world on health care issues, chiefly prevention-related issues. However, increasingly, I find myself speaking about health care economics, and specifically, health care cost containment. The ramifications of our prevention research are enormous in several respects. First, our research has led to the prevention of significant disability and pain and suffering in millions of individuals. Just as significant, the prevention of those injuries has led to major savings in health care expenditures. Unfortunately, government officials and the insurance elite completely ignore this side of the equation. They don't fund prevention related research. They don't acknowledge or call attention to and certainly don't act on the prevention research now being done. Insurance companies don't give premium reductions to those who institute preventative measures. There is a complete lack of acceptance or concern about prevention. In Vietnam, the generals didn't acknowledge the information coming back from the grunts. We face the same situation in health care.

I do not use the phrase "domestic Vietnam" loosely or in a flippant manner. Thousands of individuals made the ultimate sacrifice for our country and thousands returned alive, but wounded physically and emotionally. Unfortunately, we are repeating the past on our own shores with health care. One of the very valuable lessons I have received from the Vietnam experience was that if our policy makers and decision makers fail to listen to the grunts on the front line, you will lose the war, as we did in Vietnam. Just as Robert McNamara misled the American public (blatantly and knowingly lied to the American public, according to some), government officials and insurance industry executives are lying to the American public about the current state of health care delivery in this country. They tell us they want the delivery of quality care when in fact all they want is rationed, less than quality, cheap care.

The good news is that the grunts on the front line of health care delivery have a potential solution to the health care delivery problem. The bad news is that the generals, i.e. government bureaucrats and insurance industry executives, are not listening to us. Unfortunately, if we lose this particular war, every American citizen will become a victim. In Vietnam we could get in our helicopters and fly away. Unfortunately, if we lose this war, it will be on our own soil, and there will be no escape. Every American citizen will become a casualty. There is a solution. It involves eliminating the generals' approach of manipulating health care need and following the grunt's approach of preventing health care need. We will discuss this in some detail. But first we need to briefly digress and review how we got into the health care quagmire.

The current war in health care began almost 60 years ago during World War II when wage and price controls were introduced.

Along with wage and price controls, the government introduced employer-based health insurance, a program unique to the United States. Over the years, the employer-based health insurance programs became commonplace and the fundamental method to deliver health care benefits in America. To those with no knowledge of other health care delivery schemes, the status quo may look good. But there are major problems with employer-based health insurance. In a nutshell, these insurance programs are essentially expensive service contracts for medical service, much like a limited warranty on parts and labor, rather than a true (and more cost-effective) insurance program. In the current system, consumers and ultimately patients are insulated from prices and do not perceive the true costs of health care goods and services. Therefore, no incentive exists for patients to make cost-conscious, health care-related decisions and invest in preventative practices. Essentially each and every one of us currently goes to the health care grocery store, and picks out a bag of peas. Then we go to the checkout and the clerk tells us that bag of peas is going to cost $10,000. We look at the cashier and say, "That's fine. The person behind me has the credit card. They'll pay for it." In other words, no accountability exists in health care pricing, and this lack of accountability has led to health care costs escalating far more than they should have over the years. Furthermore, little to no physician and health care provider oversight exists. The current approach discourages prevention. Providers are paid for treating disease and injury, not for preventing them.

During flush times, the employer could bear the risk. But as prices escalated, employers naturally wanted to do whatever it took to control cost. This explains the emergence of managed care; it, supposedly, is a less costly option for employers. Government officials call this managed competition. I believe it is a form of monopolization. By the way, it's been my experience that

HMOs are low on the list; in fact, not even on the list, of those supporting preventative efforts.

So let's speed ahead to 1993 and 1994. Our president and Hillary Clinton campaigned on the need for health care reform. We should give them credit because I must say that the previous administration remained oblivious to the fact that the health care industry needed reform. In several meetings with members of the Bush administration, I found them wholly uninterested in what a grunt from the front line had to say about the problems and changes needed in health care delivery. Essentially, I was told that no problem existed in health care delivery. Some members of the administration agreed that there were problems, but they believed these to be minor. Their solution was to ask a government bureaucrat to lecture physicians and other health care providers on how they could help reduce costs by changing their practices. This individual had a health care background, but had not taken care of a patient in years. I suggested that this particular individual stuff a sock in it and listen to the grunts rather than lecture us and provide us with bogus information. My suggestion was not well received.

So the Clintons should be credited for at least recognizing that a problem exists in health care. Physicians, nurses, therapists, and every other health care providers actively taking care of patients agree with the need for reform. Unfortunately, we grunts base our belief in the need for change on drastically different premises than the Clinton Administration. Our approach focuses on prevention, the Clintons' on manipulation of health care need.

Their approach to health care reform began with putting Mrs. Clinton in charge of a 500-member health care policy development task force. To my knowledge, no health care provider actively taking care of patients served as a task force member. We grunts were disappointed, but not surprised, that the task force didn't include us. We are used to the snubs. As Yogi Berra would say, it's "deja vu all over again." The administration in essence told us front line health care providers need not apply since we are essentially special interests, and as such our views are not welcome. I would simply say that without involving the most knowledgeable individuals in a body of this nature, the policies they develop could only be, at best, fraught with misconceptions.

The task force reportedly never actually met, but it generated a document of well over a thousand pages on health care reform. This document made it clear that the administration based its major premise on manipulating health care need rather than preventing health care need.

Clinton policy wonks in Washington essentially argued for two models: (1) a state health care system similar to Canada's; and (2) an expansion of the managed care approach.

I completed a fellowship at the University of Western Ontario in London, Ontario, Canada, where I had a bird's-eye view of the Canadian health care system. I found much to appreciate in the Canadian health care delivery system, particularly the greatly diminished paperwork and administration. In our Ann Arbor office, we need to employ a dozen administrators just to fill out the hundreds of forms required by insurers. The filing space alone fills an entire room. Every medical practice in the United States incurs major overhead costs just to maintain the ever-growing paperwork. Nationwide, the cost is enormous. In Canada, health care providers need fill out only one generic form that documents that the physician saw the patient and was compensated. This results in major health care cost savings. The Canadian health care system also has outstanding doctors, nurses, and therapists who deliver high-quality health care. And that's the rub; they provide this high quality care in what I can only describe as a hostile environment, one in which the Canadian government manipulates health care costs by limiting the availability and access to care.

Just a quick example: One day I was called to the emergency room to see a patient who sustained a knee injury in the workplace. I examined this individual, and found that he had torn a cartilage in his knee. When I went back to make a clinic appointment for him, the secretary told me the first available date that a physician could see the patient would be six months later. I told the secretary the patient needed surgery. She responded that he would be scheduled for surgery following the clinic appointment and his surgery would take place somewhere between six to nine months after this appointment. In other words, this individual would be out of the workplace for anywhere between 12-18 months, during which time he would have difficulty or potentially be unable to walk and couldn't work. In the United States, an individual with a similar injury, will be back in the work place easily between six to eight weeks. The U.S. media and policy makers continue to hold up the Canadian health care system as an example we should try to emulate; they fail to address how it limits availability and access to care for everyone.

The Canadian health care system also has been held up as the epitome of an efficient, cost-effective system. However, Canada has proved less able to control health care spending than the United States. Over a 20-year time period spending rose 4.58% per year in Canada versus 4.38% in the United States. Many believe that health care in Canada is "free." My Canadian friends laugh when they hear this. They tell me that Canadians pay a tremendous surcharge in taxes for their health care delivery system. Canadians pay considerably more of their income to the government in taxes for this bureaucratic health care delivery system. We don't have to look north to Canada to see the problems with a government takeover of the health care delivery system.

We already have a microcosm of the Canadian system in place

here in the U.S. It's called the Veterans Administration health care network. Funding for Veterans' health care is fixed in each year's federal budget, and in fact, the VA has operated under global budgeting for a number of years. Global budgeting involves allocating a fixed amount of dollars over a one-year time period. When the dollars run out, services run out. The results can be devastating; e.g., last year in Ontario, the global budget ran out in December. As a result, the government shut down services and facilities and patients had to travel to Michigan for treatment. The Clinton Administration has insisted that global budgeting does not affect the practice of medicine; however, VA funding constraints based on global budgeting have led to deteriorating facilities, lower quality of care, and ultimately rationing of care. "Corners must be cut, and funds from other medical programs are cannibalized," according to John Hansen, Director of the American Legion's Commission on National Veterans' Affairs and Rehabilitation. He adds that, "The ultimate result is that which would occur in the private sector as well—rationing of care." To this, David Goreman, Assistant National Legislative Director for Medical Affairs of Disabled American Veterans, adds, "Today, and for quite some time, discretionary veteran patients are denied care. More troubling . . . those with the highest priority of care are experiencing greater difficulty receiving the care they need."

Another form of rationing of medical care currently in place in the VA medical system involves what economists call "rationing by queue." That means patients must wait for care. Surveys conducted by the Veterans Administration show a new patient must wait on average 39.6 days to see a physician in a general VA medical clinic. At the VA in my community of Ann Arbor, patients must wait at least a year for surgery. In contrast, a survey of Physician Referral Services (a physician referral network) in the Washington, DC area revealed that appointments in the private sector usually become available within a week. Lengthy waiting periods serve as a form of rationing of care that deny availability and access to care.

I have worked in the VA system, both in Chicago and in Ann Arbor. I find it less than heartwarming to see individuals that served us so well in World War II, Korea, Vietnam, the Gulf War, and many other conflicts treated in such a cold and impersonal way. From my training days, I can remember veterans were given an appointment time of either 8:00 a.m. or 1:00 p.m. They would travel in some cases several hundred miles to come to the clinic, and then would have to wait three, four, and sometimes five hours to see a physician. Many times, residents saw the veterans and they did not have the benefit of seeing attending staff physicians. I think it would be accurate to say that individuals who risk life and limb for our country receive second-class care in the VA system.

I also came to realize that some of the individuals who staff the VA hospitals prove less than top-notch. I can remember rounding one Saturday morning with our team, coming to a patient who obviously had died several hours previously; rigor mortis had set in. When our team glanced at the vital signs board, which notes the patient's temperature, blood pressure, heart rate, and breathing rate, we found that vital signs were still being recorded 15 minutes before we visited this patient. On a positive note, I believe that Dr. Ken Kizer, the VA Medical Director, is one of the most honest and visionary individuals in the field of medicine and probably the best appointment President Clinton ever made. Ken has made significant inroads in many of these problems. He's working to increase the quality of care in the VA hospitals, and to make them more patient-friendly as well as to decrease the waiting times for clinic, treatment, tests, and surgeries.

The second system bantered about in Washington as a solution to the problem is managed care. Politicians call it managed competition, but actually managed care involves nothing less than the creation of large, inefficient monopolies. Managed care monopolies pour millions of dollars into the hands of legislators in Washington and in states across the country to keep this monster alive and growing.

The creation of large inefficient monopolies is extremely shortsighted, and in the future will lead to huge increases in health care costs resulting from a lack of competition. Higher premiums and a reduction in quality and services will become the norm. A couple of years ago, a labor union representing more than 30,000 employees of Kaiser Permanente testified before Congress that the nation's biggest HMO is charging its enrollees increasingly higher premiums and turning away nonmembers seeking emergency services. Aetna recently reached a settlement with the Texas attorney general for $10 million in a case where it was alleged the insurance company penalized physicians who refused to deny care to patients. This story has been repeated time and again across the U.S.

Managed care also leads to higher administrative costs. One 1996 study in the *New England Journal of Medicine* reported that states with higher managed care enrollments had significantly higher administrative costs. These administrative costs accounted for 25.6% of the total cost of health care delivered. For private health insurance claims, the adminstrative cost was 11.2%. The administrative costs associated with medical savings accounts was 1.5%. The authors of the study concluded that no evidence exists that managed care will prune hospital administrative costs. The findings of this report have been widely supported in the medical literature.

Some of the cost-cutting schemes of managed care companies would be downright laughable if they were not so antithetical to sound medical advice and the interests of good patient care. It was widely reported by the network news media in late 1999 that certain managed care companies would not pay for ambulance visits resulting from 911 calls. If an emergency arose in a patient's home, they would have to call an 800 number and answer an 18-point questionnaire over the phone. If the administrator deemed the answers appropriate, he or she would send an ambulance to the person's home. One can only imagine the nightmare scenarios that will develop as an individual responds to question 15 while their husband or wife is in the midst of a crushing heart attack, only to succumb while the insurance bureaucrat asks question 16, 17, and 18.

The federal employee health benefit plan (FEHBP) provides an example of what to expect from managed care reform packages. FEHBP offers guaranteed insurance through an intermediary, the Federal Office of Personnel Management. Four and one-half million employees and retirees of the government are eligible for FEHBP and have their choice of traditional fee-for-service policies or managed care plans.

A review of the economic and patient track record of the system dashes the hopes of government officials and belies their misguided beliefs. Despite the clout the office of personnel management exerts, its spending has consistently escalated over the past 10-year period. Expenditures have increased by 179% overall since 1982 and by 155% on a per person basis. After adjusting for inflation, the per person premium cost increased by 76% over 10 years. By comparison, the nation's total health care expenditure increased 73% over the same time period after adjusting for inflation.

The government accounting office found the FEHBP plan cost to benefit ratio to be 51% more than the average cost/benefit ratio for large, insured, nonfederal programs, such as businesses in municipal governments and 89% more than the ratio for large self-insured businesses. In another report, the government accounting office found the FEHBP program to be "highly vulnerable" to fraud and abuse.

I could list a litany of the negative experiences I have encountered trying to provide quality health care to individuals who belonged to managed care plans. I recently saw a patient who fell on the ice while skating in northern Michigan and dislocated his shoulder. He was visiting from out of town and alone; his wife remained home. So he drove himself to the emergency room, knowing that he had a very serious injury to his shoulder. His arm was numb, and he could not move it other than to keep it tucked to his side. He finally arrived at a small community hospital. He checked in and informed the staff that he belonged to a managed care organization not based in northern Michigan. A hospital representative contacted the managed care company. He returned to tell the injured man that the managed care company found his problem "nonlife-threatening"; if he wanted a physician to take care of the problem, he would have to pay the emergency room visit and all fees out of his own pocket. This individual did not have any money with him since he had left his wallet at home while he went skating. Since he could not pay for his visit and rather than run up a bill, he elected to drive himself home.

By driving with a dislocated shoulder, this individual took his own life and the life of others in his hands. After he returned home, he contacted his family physician, who saw him several days later. Following x-rays, the physician told him that he had a small bruise to his shoulder and had possibly injured a muscle. The physician did not refer him to a specialist and didn't recognize the dislocated shoulder. The patient put up a brave front, but his wife said at night she would hear him crying in pain from his shoulder injury. This continued for two months. After several more visits, his family physician finally referred this individual to me. I took two x-rays and they told the story. He had dislocated his shoulder at the time of his skating fall and essentially went without treatment for two months. As a result, he damaged more soft tissue around the shoulder. This could well have adversely affected his arm function over the long-term. I'm sure that his family physician, like most family physicians, is a wonderful, highly dedicated, very intelligent individual; however, to ask a family physician to know everything about every medical problem goes beyond asking the impossible. In some cases, they need to refer problems to specialists. However, managed care entities across the U.S. in effect ask the impossible by requiring family physicians to serve as the gatekeepers to care. As the gate-keeper, the family physician is asked to make the decision about who sees a specialist. Family physicians are discouraged and in some cases even punished for providing treatment or referring patients to specialists. This places a tremendous burden on family physicians and sometimes leads to scenarios such as the dislocated shoulder incident described above. Similar incidents occur across the U.S., and should no longer occur in silence. Those who refer too much, who order tests, who order newer medicines, who go the extra step for their patients, are punished by the insurance companies. In our community, a managed care company recently sent family physicians a bill at the end of the year asking them to pay back for their "overusage" of the system.

Managed care companies often discourage treatment. For example, administrators from a managed care company recently suggested that I stop prescribing antiinflammatory medications. As a practicing orthopedic surgeon and shoulder specialist, about 95 to 99% of the individuals I take care of have a chronic, inflammatory shoulder condition. The most effective way to treat this condition is with antiinflammatories, icing, and a physical therapy program. The administrators told me that the antiinflammatories I prescribe cost the managed care company too much money. They asked me to stop prescribing these medications and use an over-the-counter, less effective medicine that the patient would pay for directly. I refused to do so and they told me that if I kept prescribing the medications, I would be" deselected." That's a fancy way of saying that I would be thrown out of the managed care company. I would no longer be given the opportunity to care for the patients who asked for and needed my services. The administrators who initiated this policy were not physicians or nurses. They had never taken care of a patient. They basically had no functional medical knowledge.

Unfortunately, this occurs with managed care companies throughout the US. MBAs and bureaucrats with no functional medical knowledge attempt to coerce highly-trained, dedicated, health care professionals into denying care. In some cases, the health care professional resists the coercion and does what's best for the patient. Unfortunately, and all too frequently, the sanctions are severe enough that physicians succumb to the bureaucrat's economic demands and deliver less than high quality care. I can find no better way to describe the managed care system than an HMO executive did in the *Wall Street Journal* on June 18, 1997. "We see people as numbers, not patients," he said. "We're a mass-production, medical assembly line, and there is no room for the human equation in our bottom line. Profits are king." Unfortunately, this has become the mantra for HMO executives throughout the US. As Milton Friedman has said, "The power to do good is also the power to do harm."

Managed care is a bureaucratic nightmare and I find it most disconcerting that the Clinton health care plan would have introduced more bureaucracy into the health care system. The plan would create 59 new federal agencies, expand the role of 20 federal agencies, and introduce 79 new federal mandates. A mandate is a directive by the federal government to states and localities to provide service; however, the federal government does not provide the monetary support for their mandates. So states and localities are forced to raise taxes to cover the services required by the federal government. Of all these federal agencies created under this plan, not one of them focused on the most cost-effective means for cutting health care expenditures; i.e., prevention. In fact, the plan left prevention completely out of the equation.

It's easy to look at a flawed health care plan based on flawed premises and flawed models and tear it to shreds. The difficulty comes in developing an alternative that truly would prove effective for the patient. If you want to create effective health care reform, you really only have to answer one question. Does the patient benefit? If the answer is yes, the proposed plan becomes viable; if the answer is no, then the proposal needs to be dropped. The Institute is fortunate to have a board of directors that has reviewed health care reform plans and developed a practical approach to health care cost containment based on prevention. This approach could be implemented without hardship to the general public in a very cost-effective manner. Every member of our board of directors has many years of clinical medical experience and serves on the frontline of health care delivery. Our proposal for health care cost containment includes the following eight points:

1. Billions of dollars in health care costs could be eliminated through federal government-led advancement of prevention efforts. Prevention research continues to be underemphasized and underfunded by all government agencies throughout the United States. One measure would be to give tax incentives to corporations and individuals that institute prevention methods recommended by the Center for Disease Control or the National Center for Injury Prevention and Control.

2. We need to place more emphasis on injury-prevention research. Injury in America remains the most underrecognized, major public health problem facing the nation today. Injury is the single, greatest killer of Americans ages 1-44 and costs the nation

more than 150 billion dollars annually. Furthermore, 62 million Americans require medical attention annually to treat injuries. If we implemented the recommendations from one prevention study performed at our Institute (the breakaway base study), we could prevent 1.7 million injuries and save 2 billion dollars in associated health care costs annually (according to the Centers for Disease Control & Prevention). We spent $1,000 for that particular study. This demonstrates how a small outlay of funds can lead to enormous benefits in reducing injury and associated health care costs. Yet not one of the 59 new federal agencies created by the Clinton health care plan had an ounce to do with prevention.

3. We need to curtail unhealthy habits of the general public which lead to unnecessary and expensive health care costs. Smoking, alcohol abuse, and the use of firearms lead to an increased incidence of disease and diminish productivity while raising health care costs. One way to curtail these habits is to heavily tax these products.

4. More than one-quarter of health care costs could be cut by eliminating the multitude of paperwork required by the insurance industry. Switching to an electronic billing system would eliminate billions of dollars in health care expenditures annually. A recent study in the *New England Journal of Medicine* showed that we could save 50 billion dollars annually by switching from the current paperwork-laden system to an electronic billing system.

5. Insurance industry administrative costs must be curtailed. The layers upon layers of insurance company bureaucracy continue to usurp billions of dollars in health care costs each year. A recent study showed that over the past five years, the health care system has added three and one-half administrators for every health care provider (doctors, nurses, therapists, trainers). As I noted, the Canadian health care system has significantly diminished the burden of paperwork. It also has significantly reduced the role of

administrators. A recent study found that the health care system in Alberta, Canada meets the health care needs of two and one-half million individuals with only 150 administrators. In contrast, Blue Cross/Blue Shield of Massachusetts requires over 6,000 administrators to cover the health care needs of a like number of two and one-half million people.

Furthermore, health care executives receive compensation significantly out of proportion to their performance. The chairman of New York's Blue Cross/Blue Shield Plan, for example, grosses $600,000 annually. Blue Cross/Blue Shield of New York has a fleet of 123 cars and its offices house $130,000 in art and sculpture and $62,832 in silk plants. The chief executive has a $48,000 security system in his office. (Who's he protecting himself from? Irate patients?) This despite the fact that Blue Cross/Blue Shield of New York has posted a $255 million loss since 1990. Insurance administrators throughout the US receive high compensation despite similar losses. These administrative costs are breaking the system and driving some insurers bankrupt. In 1989, New Hampshire regulators had to intervene when the state's Blue Cross/Blue Shield exhausted its cash reserves. West Virginia's Blue Cross/Blue Shield ran out of money five years ago. Blue Cross of Washington DC posted losses of $182 million over seven years. The net worth of Maryland's Blue Cross Plan dropped from $122 million to $25 million in seven years. Nevertheless, the chief executive officer of Maryland's Blue Cross Plan receives an annual compensation of $775,000. These figures, however, are dwarfed by total compensation packages provided to the CEO's of HMO's. In 2001 the CEO of United Health Group was compensated $29,154,675.00. One would think this would be an exorbitant salary until one compares his salary with Health South CEO's salary. Health South is one of the largest HMO's in the country. The total compensation package for the CEO in

2001 was $129,199,197.00. The recipe for an exorbitant salary of this nature is simple: deny availability and access to care by people paying premiums and deny and short change payment to the providers in the healthcare delivery system

6. The state legislative process requiring a certificate of need (CON) for medical equipment needs to be eliminated. In many states, if an entity, such as a hospital or a group of individuals, wants to implement the use of a CT scanner, they must obtain a certificate of need. This approval process can cost hundreds of thousands of dollars, escalating health care costs and, in effect reducing competition and creating inefficient, large monopolies that further drive up costs. A Wharton School of Business analysis of CONs noted that hospitals tend to dominate CONs, using them to block access into the marketplace and restrict competition from ambulatory surgical centers, radiology facilities, and any entity that does testing or treats patients. The Wharton study concluded that CONs restrict the supply of health care and lead to higher prices.

7. We must decrease the number of disease entities insurance policies are required to cover. When mandated coverage for these entities increases (including coverage for elective procedures such as cosmetic plastic surgery), the costs of insurance policies escalate drastically. In 1970, state legislatures mandated that insurance companies cover 48 particular disease entities; however, by 1990, state legislatures mandated coverage for over 1,000 disease entities, Over 30% of individuals currently uninsured could be insured if state requirements were dropped.

8. Tort reform must be instituted immediately. Unfortunately, the vast majority of legislators happen to be attorneys, and to expect attorneys to police themselves is beyond a pipe dream. We could save billions of dollars in health care costs if we instituted tort reform on a national basis by implementing arbitration boards

on a widespread basis. Lawsuits against physicians more than tripled over the past four years. It's been estimated that the resulting defensive medicine practiced by physicians, e.g., ordering unnecessary tests to "cover all bases," has increased health care expenses $15 billion annually.

The question remains: what vehicle can deliver the necessary changes we need in health care? The most effective vehicle for instituting our proposed changes and delivering a more efficient, cost-effective health care system is the institution of medical savings accounts. We believe that the cost for this coherent, comprehensive approach would be minimal compared to the costs for plans currently proposed in Washington. Medical savings accounts give cost control incentives directly to consumers. They also stimulate true market-cost-controlled competition. Medical savings accounts will provide high quality health care and allow consumer choice. The doctor and patient once again become a team, deciding between themselves what treatment is necessary and most cost-effective. With medical savings accounts, individuals can set aside a portion of their earnings in a tax-free investment account similar to current retirement IRAs. A part of the money would pay for a high-deductible, low-premium insurance to cover mostly catastrophic events. The money not used for insurance can accumulate tax free until retirement. Individuals could pay for small medical bills out-of-pocket. Medical savings accounts also have the added benefit of being portable, i.e., your health insurance stays with you when you leave your job. With retirees, the government pays for this high deductible policy.

A study from the Mackinac Center for Public Policy, a public policy think tank in Michigan, found that widespread use of medical savings accounts would cut as much as $200 billion from the annual US health care bill. Some of this savings would accrue as a result of preventive measures that it would stimulate; e.g., mammograms, well baby checks, and routine annual physicals. More people would select these preventive services in an attempt to save more money in their savings account. I know of no other mechanism that actually increases the use of preventive care. Several corporations throughout the United States have implemented the medical savings account approach with outstanding results. For example, Golden Rule Insurance Company based in Indianapolis, Indiana offered medical savings accounts to its 1,300 employees. By the second year, 90% of the employees had enrolled in the plan and health care costs declined by 40%. Furthermore, Golden Rule employees increased their use of preventive care; 20% of them reported using their MSA funds to purchase a preventive service they would not have bought under a traditional, health-insurance policy.

Dominion Resources, an energy company on the Atlantic Coast, offered medical savings accounts to its 200 employees. After one year, 80% of its employees had enrolled in the plan. Since implementing the program, health care costs at Dominion Resources have increased by less than 1% annually; health care costs for other corporations based in the state of Virginia increased 20% annually. Three years into the program, Dominion found it had spent 33% less than its projected health care budget.

Several studies on medical savings accounts have found them to be effective in reducing health care costs and increasing preventative care. They reduce administrative costs drastically because there are no administrative costs for small claims; these are paid out-of-pocket. Medical savings accounts potentially could save $33 billion in administrative costs annually. The RAND Corporation reviewed medical savings accounts and found that the reduced expenditures do not lead to individuals foregoing necessary health care. They found health care outcomes under medical savings accounts identical to outcomes under traditional insurance. The savings resulted from a reduction in the use of optional services and more cost-based selection between providers, as well as increased use of preventive care.

Utilizing the medical savings account vehicle as a means of obtaining a cost-effective, rational, and equitable means of reforming our health care system would serve every American equally and efficiently. It therefore makes both economic and medical sense.

I had the opportunity to share this information with the staff of then-majority leader Bob Dole. As we all know, the 1994 Clinton health care plan proved unpopular and played a role in the Congressional turnover from a Democratic to a Republican majority. Despite this defeat, the 1995 version of health care reform took on the air of "Been there, done that." This version involved changes in Medicare that essentially placed recipients in one of three plans. The first two plans would either raise recipients' deductibles and copayments or place them into a managed care organization; in other words, a rationed care, cut costs approach. A proposed third approach would institute medical savings accounts. Medical savings accounts would, as we've shown, empower health care consumers by giving them direct incentives to control costs. This alternative would maintain health care quality and consumer choice. Unfortunately, the medical savings account proposal never left the Senate. During the debate, Senate Democrats, led by Senator Exon of Nebraska, removed medical savings accounts as an option for Medicare recipients, thereby forcing them into managed care programs and rationed medical care. In other words, they achieved the same end as that proposed in the 1994 Clinton health care plan.

Senator Exon pulled medical savings accounts off the table by citing the "Byrd rule." This removes measures that do not contribute to deficit reduction; not a bad rule if it's based on accurate data. Senator Exon's data was, to say the least, bogus. He based his action on a congressional budget office report that assumed only 1% of seniors would choose medical savings accounts if they were instituted. The report also assumed medical savings accounts would increase seniors' out-of-pocket expenses. These assumptions did not take into account the experience of the more than 1,000 corporations that had instituted medical savings accounts. These corporations had found that the vast majority of their employees used MSAs within the first year, significantly higher than 60% rather than the 1% predicted by the budget office. The report overlooked the out-of-pocket expenses for copayments and deductibles that seniors now pay, roughly $1,200 a year on average. With standard medical savings accounts, the most out-of-pocket expense a senior could incur would be $1,000 a year. This represents a 17% reduction in costs over the current situation. Furthermore, the government now pays $4,800 per senior annually. With medical savings accounts, the government would pay only $3,300 per senior annually, a 31% reduction in cost.

To Senator Dole's credit, he went to bat for medical savings accounts and introduced them back into the health care proposal on a more limited basis. Corporations with 50 or fewer employees and self-insured individuals can use Medical savings accounts. That's great for these folks, but what about the majority of Americans that could truly benefit by this health care approach? Unfortunately, even today, very few of us have heard of medical savings accounts, and this is to the detriment of the American public. Medical savings accounts are the most cost-effective means of reducing health care expenditures and the only health care reform plan that encourages prevention. Victor Hugo has said, "Greater than the tread of mighty armies is an idea whose time has come." I believe that the time has come for medical savings accounts.

CHAPTER TWELVE

The Making of a Life

"You make a living by what you get, you make a life by what you give."

—WINSTON CHURCHILL

While training to make a living in my chosen profession of medicine, I actually ended up making a life. My journey as a physician began over 30 years ago with my volunteer work at a local community hospital in the suburbs of Chicago. This work involved transporting patients and working in a pharmacy. I learned health care from the trenches and that's the best way to learn a profession. This from-the-bottom-up approach allowed me to interact with patients on a more personal basis and thus has helped me provide a higher quality of care. Through this experience, I also came to know the therapists, nurses, nurse aides, radiology technicians, and physicians who make up the health care system and to understand their dedication.

My journey then took me to Bucknell University in Lewisburg, Pennsylvania where I earned a Bachelor of Arts Degree majoring in chemistry and economics. During my breaks between semesters and over the summer, I continued my volunteer work in cancer research programs and orthopedic programs. I worked with Dr. Raoul Fresco, a dedicated pathologist and researcher who emigrated from Egypt because of political persecution in Egypt. A true renaissance man, he paid for his medical education by serving as a music critic on local radio stations. I also worked with Dr. Israel Davidson, a leading cancer researcher, and Drs. Hampar and Armen Kelikian, two of the most brilliant clinicians I have known. The Kelikians were responsible for my going into the field of orthopedic surgery. I was assigned to their services. Hampar reconstructed Bob Dole's arm when he returned injured from WWII. In fact, I met Bob Dole for the first time when I served as a volunteer in the Kelikians' clinic in 1978. By working with the Kelikians, I came to understand that becoming an outstanding clinician takes more than a grasp of science and of data; it takes energy, enthusiasm, dedication and a commitment to the art of medicine and to people. The Kelikians initiated my career in orthopedics and taught me what it takes to give and deliver high quality orthopedic care. If not for the guidance of Dr. Bill Larmon (who introduced me to Dr. Hampar and Armen Kelikian) I believe I probably would not have been admitted to Northwestern University Medical School in Chicago, let alone become a practicing orthopedic surgeon.

My travels after Northwestern took me to Ann Arbor and the University of Michigan Medical School where I completed a five year internship and residency in orthopedic surgery. As I've noted previously, the residency seemed to take a lifetime to complete. It was like a five year boot camp. Despite the challenge, I learned that no matter what's thrown at me, I will survive and persevere. Residency taught me mental and physical toughness. Without the help of Dr. Bob Hensinger I truly believe I wouldn't have become the capable orthopedic surgeon I believe I am today. He taught me the fundamentals of how to become a quality physician and surgeon and, by way of example, he taught me how to practice the art of medicine.

Finally, my journey took me to London, Ontario, Canada, where I studied under the direction of Dr. Richard J. Hawkins, one of the preeminent shoulder surgeons in the world. Hawk taught me how to maintain a balance between my personal and professional life. That wasn't taught in medical school or residency training. I truly was blessed by having outstanding mentors at every phase of my professional development.

Many people ask me why I decided to become a doctor. Obviously it takes many years of work at tremendous expense to your family, and you spend some of the best years of your life studying while others are enjoying life. My standard answer to this question has always been that I enjoy science, I enjoy people, and I feel that medicine provides the best mix of both. That answer, while true, doesn't tell the whole story. Three very significant events in my life led me to pursue a career in medicine.

The first occurred when I was 12 years old. My grandmother, who lived with us, became acutely ill. Like my parents, my grandmother was one of my best friends. She lived with us my entire life and we grew very close. Every night before bedtime, she told me stories about the good old days. She introduced me to all the family members I never met. Early one morning, she complained of tremendous pain in her abdomen. She also had difficulty breathing, something that had never troubled her before. I knew that something was very wrong. My parents called an ambulance and the ambulance took her to the hospital where her longtime physician practiced.

Three days later, my grandmother died. I remember the day like it was yesterday. My neighbors dropped me off from school and I walked to the door. Just then, my mom drove up with my dad following behind her in another car. They told me that my grandmother, my friend, had died an hour earlier. I was devastated. The worse part was that I never said goodbye. A second blood clot had traveled to her lungs and she died immediately. In retrospect, it appears that she had developed a clot on that morning when she became so acutely ill. Unfortunately, her physician didn't discover this and, consequently, didn't give her the appropriate blood thinning medicines that would have saved her life.

At the time of her death, I was scheduled to compete in the state science competition in Champaign/Urbana at the University of Illinois, my parents' alma mater. The year previously I had entered the science competition and had come in second place, which my parents and grandmother considered an excellent accomplishment for a seventh grader. It wasn't enough as far as I was concerned. My grandmother's funeral took place on the day that the science competition was to be held. I wanted to attend the funeral and didn't want to travel to Champaign. But my parents sat me down and gently persuaded me to go because that's what my grandmother would have wanted. That day, at the ripe old age of 12, I dedicated myself to two goals—to win the science competition for my grandmother and to become a physician, a physician who would not make the mistakes that led to my grandmother's death.

My aunts Evelyn and Mamie took me to the University of Illinois and, during the trip, did everything they could to cheer me up. They tried very hard, but they just couldn't quite succeed. I spent the next two days in Champaign feeling miserable the whole time. I did win the state competition and my science project continued for another four years. By the time I graduated from high school, my work on this project led to me being named one of the top 40 science students in the country. It was obvious to me that Grandmother Mae Janda was watching out for me from above both in Champaign, Illinois as an eighth grader and in Washington DC as a senior in high school, and to this day I continue to dedicate myself and my work to her memory.

The second event that led to my becoming a physician concerned my dad's very close cousin, and my second cousin, George. He seemed more like an uncle to me. During my freshman year in high school, George was diagnosed with inoperable lung cancer, undoubtedly due to his long history of smoking. I can never remember George without a pack of Lucky Strikes in his pocket and a Lucky Strike in his mouth. I found it ironic that something that could cause such harm should have the name "Lucky."

One night my mom and dad brought me to the hospital to see George, who was having some difficulty breathing. During the visit, George asked me to sit on the bed next to him. "Shorty," he said. He used to like to call me Shorty—even as a freshman in high school when I grew to be about four inches taller than he was. "I'm dying of lung cancer because I smoked cigarettes. I started smoking when I was young and all the advertisements told me that smoking would be good for me and make me grow bigger and stronger. Do two things for me. One, never ever smoke. It will kill you. Two, I think you should think about becoming a doctor. Your dad is very successful in the construction business. What he does benefits a tremendous number of people, but I believe you can build your life around people in a different manner and have a very positive effect on their lives if you become a physician." This had a profound impact on my becoming a physician and on my interest in prevention.

It's ironic. Roughly 27 years after George spoke these words, a good friend of mine gave me a cigarette advertisement from a 1946 issue of *Life* magazine. It listed the benefits of smoking and said that smoking cigarettes could prevent disease. My friend, Jerry Klein, gave me that article because he knew of my experiences with some sports equipment manufacturers and the false claims they had made; he didn't know about the conversation I had with George 27 years previously.

The third reason why I became a physician concerns my family. "The family is one of nature's masterpieces," according to George Santayana *(A Life of Reason)*. If that's the case, my family is truly a Monet, Renoir, and a Picasso all rolled into one. Without the help and guidance and support of my parents, Ben and Ruth Janda, I could not have accomplished what I have in my life. My grandmother, my aunts, my uncles all guided me, helped me, supported me, and were there when I needed assistance.

My wife, Libby, truly has been a godsend to me. She has withstood the trying times of a very difficult residency and lengthy absences during my fellowship where we lived several hundred miles apart days on end. (I commuted to and from London Ontario, Canada and Ann Arbor.) She has been with me every step of the way in the founding, development, failures and successes of the Institute. She has never questioned the time and the effort that I donate to the Institute or to my clinical practice or my patients. She has helped through the years with the Institute symposium and auction and other projects. And, most of all, she's given her time and effort to the most frustrating client in her legal career—me. As I noted previously, when you become a physician you lose a large part of your life and your freedom. Outside the office, the beeper is always going off and the phone is always ringing with one of your patients or friends calling to seek medical advice. Most physicians' spouses become frustrated by the continued interference in your private life and the lack of freedom in a life devoted to medicine. Not Libby. As the song goes, she truly has been the wind beneath my wings.

Our children, Allison and Katie truly served as my inspiration for the Institute. When I held a sick Allison in my arms that very hot and humid July 1989 morning, I grew more determined that if I could ever do anything in my life to prevent other parents from facing a similar, if not worse, circumstance, I would do so. Allison and Katie have always pitched in and helped with the auctions and the symposiums and anything to do with the Institute. And they're involved in other charitable causes; e.g., last year Allison ran in a mile run to benefit breast cancer victims. They are wonderful children who, at the ripe old ages of 12 and 10, truly have become young adults. They are happy, intelligent, giving, and most of all caring people who I hope have learned by example that you make a life by what you give.

At one point, the Institute began to receive threatening phone calls and I grew concerned about my family's welfare. So I sat Allison and Katie down and talked to them about the situation. Even though very young, they grasped the nature of these threats. Nonetheless, they both looked at me and said in unison, "Daddy, what you're doing helps kids. We want you to keep helping kids." From the mouth of babes.

Both Allison and Katie are outstanding students, piano players, and outstanding athletes in their own right. They both love the sports of golf and soccer. It's interesting how two people very similar in many respects can have such different personalities. I realize all parents see this in their offspring. One expression of this difference is how they play soccer. Allison is fast on her feet, maneuvers the ball quickly and always passes off for someone else to kick the goal. Katie, on the other hand, while fast on her feet, seems to be the Wayne Gretzky who positions herself in front of the goal to knock it home.

I also find it interesting to see them battle adversity on the soccer field. If Katie finds a player not abiding by the rules, her first step is to tell that player to follow the rules. If that doesn't work, she tells the ref. If that doesn't work, Katie takes matters into her own hands. Allison, on the other hand, will let the offending player continue her misguided efforts for a while. But at some point, she reaches a boiling point and puts an end to it. I will always remember when a rather large girl on the other team, almost twice the size of the other girls, began throwing down players on Allison's team. The referee refused to call a penalty. After one of her teammates got hurt, Allison went up to the girl and told her to stop her antics. The next time down the field that girl tackled Allison and stepped on her face. Allison didn't cry. She just got up, readjusted her glasses, and kept playing. The next time the large girl dribbled the ball down the field, out of nowhere, speedy Allison flew at the girl with her elbow held high. Allison hit the girl in the chest and knocked her over. She stood over the girl, pointed at her and said, "I told you to stop hurting people."

I also find it interesting that whenever either girl lays the wood to the other team, the other parents look at me; they never seem to look at my wife, Libby. I'm very proud of our two girls. My only hope is that I can be half the parent or even one-tenth the parent that my parents have been to me.

So in the process of training to become a physician, I ended up making a life for myself and hopefully for others. I believe I made my life by giving my time and my efforts to help others and to prevent injury. To this day, well over 11 years after that fateful morning in July 1989, I cannot explain what happened in that hospital room at the University of Michigan. But it changed the course of my life.

Once again, Ralph Waldo Emerson has said, "God himself does not speak prose, but communicates with us by hints, omens, inferences and dark resemblances in objects lying all around us." I truly believe that He was communicating with me on that July morning. The Institute and my life's work grew out of that event. On that morning, I cut a deal for the health of my daughter that I would continue my research and I would establish an Institute focusing on that prevention. My journey with the Institute has been remarkable and, at times, frustrating. However, the true message that I'd like to leave you with, the message embodied in the Institute, is that an individual, a single individual can make a difference for people. I don't like the slogan, "It takes a village to raise a child." It suggests to me that only a bureaucratic entity, government, or a corporation or industry can make a difference for people. I believe the lesson of the Institute is that one small organization, a small group of people, or even a single individual can make an enormous impact. That's not to say that the journey has been without frustration and at times led me to question whether we should continue our efforts. But we've persevered. Our work at the Institute has become a case study in perseverance and dedication.

When things get tough, I remember Ralph Waldo Emerson's words: "Bad times have a scientific value. These are occasions a good learner would not miss." *(Conduct of Life.)* Ben Janda's philosophy that if you turn lemons into lemonade, things will always work out for the best, has yet to be proved wrong.

In these pages, I have taken you with me on the journey from the inception of the Institute to where we are today. Injuries continue to occur, health care expenditures continue to be spent needlessly. So our efforts and our journey continues. We each have our own journey and a vessel to carry us on that journey. My hope is that as you embark on your journey, you carefully survey the scene and turn your observations into actions that will benefit your fellow human beings. Take a page from this book and from Norman Vaughn's.

DREAM BIG AND DARE TO FAIL!

Prevention Checklist for Parents, Grandparents, and Community Leaders

- Are the coaches in your community knowledgeable in conditioning and training techniques for the particular age group concerned?

- Are the coaches well versed in CPR techniques and AED use?

- Are the coaches certified?

- Has your student athlete had a preparticipation physical examination?

- Are Automatic External Defibrillators (AED's) available at all fields, gymnasiums, and sports arenas in your community?

- Do your softball and baseball fields **all** have breakaway bases?

- Are the youngest student athletes in your local baseball leagues training with lighter weight baseballs?

- Are the batting helmets used at **all** times when batting, running bases, and in the on-deck circle?

- Are face shields attached to **all** helmets being used?

- Are there padded goalposts on **all** soccer fields in your community?

- Are soccer shin guards used at **all** soccer practices and games?

- Are heading drills in soccer using a light-mass beach ball instead of a standard soccer ball?

- Are you, the parent, grandparent, or community activist, confident that **all** student athletes are wearing well-fitted and up-to-date equipment?

- Are hockey helmets worn in **all** hockey practices and games?

- Are full-face shields attached to all hockey helmets?

- Are field officials rigorously enforcing the rulebook of the particular sport concerned?

- Are helmets **mandatory for every family member** while biking, ice-skating, roller-skating, roller-blading, skate boarding, sledding, and skiing?

- Is the equipment in interscholastic sports such as football being tested for maximum protective standards (e.g., Snell standard for football helmets)?

- Is recreational sports equipment stored in a safe place so younger children do not inadvertently hurt themselves or others (e.g., golf clubs)?

- Do you, a responsible parent, grandparent, or guardian, take the time and effort to occasionally monitor your student athlete's practices to determine if the practices are safe from a physical and psychological standpoint?

APPENDIX TWO

Injury Statistics
for 2000 – 2002

National Electronic Injury Surveillance System 2000 – 2002
Summary Report—E.R. Visits

Sport/Activity	Number of Injuries		
	2000	2001	2002
Baseball / Softball	308,944	301,116	304,543
Basketball	600,256	653,661	615,546
Bowling	22,890	22,933	21,133
Boxing	13,704	11,506	11,811
Diving	12,014	11,196	11,050
Football	399,501	414,607	387,948
Golf	45,064	46,089	39,740
Gymnastics	37,583	33,700	29,678
Ice Hockey	60,356	53,922	65,882
Inline Skating	90,164	69,174	60,572
Lacrosse	7,457	8,383	8,068
Playground Climbing	81,060	87,444	126,622
Soccer	185,064	175,470	173,519
Sledding	38,546	23,186	24,998
Skateboarding	86,781	56,671	113,192
Snowboarding	56,254	64,523	63,014
Snow Skiing	94,883	89,885	90,285
Tennis	24,231	24,885	19,633
Trampolines	100,303	91,870	89,393
4-Wheel ATV's	84,900	111,700	113,900
Wrestling	52,797	53,791	36,702

APPENDIX THREE

Dehydration

Over the past 6 years, twenty-three student athletes succumbed to heat-related deaths. Some very logical and easily implemented guidelines could completely alleviate fatalities related to heat stroke. As immediate past chairman of the Sports Injury Advisory Group to the Governor of the State of Michigan, Mr. John Engler, our group developed a number of recommendations related to football—but they could be easily applied to every sport and recreational activity.

These recommendations include:

- Acclimatize to heat gradually. Early practices, such as the first 7-10 days, should be shorter and less intense, as should practices on abnormally hot or humid days. In addition athletes should be encouraged to initiate their own conditioning program several months prior to the beginning of the season. During the hottest weather practice sessions should be scheduled in cooler parts of the day.

- Both the temperature and relative humidity should be taken into account in determining the length of practice sessions. It has been suggested that if the sum of the temperature and relative humidity are greater than or equal to 160, precautions must be taken. If the sum is greater than 180, practice and or games should be cancelled.

- Adjust the activity level and provide frequent rest periods during hot weather. Rest should be accomplished in shaded areas, helmets removed, and jerseys should be loosened or removed. In addition, rest periods should consist of 15 minutes each hour of workout.

- Cold water should be available in unlimited quantities to players. Scheduled water breaks should be strictly enforced.

- Salt should be replaced through salting of food, not salt tablets.

- Athletes should be weighed before and after each practice to monitor water loss. Weight loss greater than 3% indicates a substantial risk and 5% a significant danger to the student athlete.

- During practice athletes should wear cooling clothing such as shorts and fish net jerseys. Sweat saturated t-shirts should be changed often because they do retain heat. Helmets should only be used sparingly in hot weather.

- Parental involvement, such as observing practices, should be done on a rotating basis between all the parents of the student athletes. A monitor for practices, as well as game situations, can only lead to potentially alleviating this ultra tragic scenario of heat illness.

- It should be noted that some athletes are more susceptible to heat illness. Identify and observe closely those at greatest risk of heat illness, including those that are poorly conditioned, overweight, have an acute illness, have cystic fibrosis, diabetes, or mental retardation. In addition, student athletes that have a previous history of heat illness should be watched closely during practices and hot weather.

- It is imperative that all coaches, parents, and players be on the lookout for this all-too-common scenario. Any athlete showing signs of fatigue, lethargy, inattention, stupor, and/ or awkwardness should be immediately removed from participation, cooled down, and placed in a shaded environment.

- A general rule of thumb I suggest to prevent dehydration:

  Before Activity: 2 –16 ounce cups of water 2 hours
                             prior to participation.

  During Activity: 8 oz water (1/2 of a 16 oz. water bottle)
                             every 30-45 minutes.

  After Activity: 3 cups of water for every pound
                            lost during activity.

With implementation of the above eleven steps, I believe the occurrence of heat illness would be eliminated. However, it is mandatory that parents become more activists in their student-athletes practices and games to make sure that the fatal scenario that we have seen across the country does not occur in our own backyards.

APPENDIX FOUR

Chest Impact Injuries – Automatic External Defibrillators – *The Oprah Factor*

The most common reason for children dying in sports-related activities is from an impact to the chest with either a baseball, hockey puck, lacrosse ball or some other object. Over the past four years over 125 individuals have died due to an impact to the chest. As I have pointed out in Chapter 7: Not All that Glitters is Gold, the timing of the impact is the critical event which leads to this scenario. If the impact occurs at the "exact" phase of the heart cycle this could send the heart into shock and make it beat wildly. The heart will beat so wildly it cannot pump blood effectively to the other vital organs and that is how these children die. As I point out in the book, softer heavier baseballs, and chest protectors do not completely protect this scenario from developing. Lighter weight baseballs do reduce the risk of injury and fatality, however, they do not completely protect the child from this rare, but catastrophic event. If this scenario develops, the most important steps to take include: 1) Call 911 and initiate CPR and 2) Deliver a shock to the chest in order to "shock the heart into it's normal rhythm" **within 2–4** minutes of the child being hit. The two ways to deliver that shock are either a thump to the chest or better yet, use of an Automatic External Defibrillator (AED). While CPR may help prolong the window of survival, it cannot restore a normal heart rhythm. For every minute that goes by without defibrillation, a cardiac arrest victim's chances of survival decreases by about 10%. **Automatic External Defibrillators should be on every field, and in every gymnasium, hockey rink, and sports complex throughout the country.** An AED could save someone's life.

There are a number of Automatic External Defibrillators on the market. We at the Institute have concluded that the most effective AED device should:

- Uses Biphasic Waveform.
- Be approved to be placed on a conscious victim, either adult or pediatric and cleared by the F.D.A. to treat victims of all ages.
- Have live scenario training options with comprehensive voice commands.
- Have Non-Invasive 3 lead monitoring.
- Be safe in water and metal surfaces.
- Detect artifact noise, motions, environment and radio.
- Take only 15 seconds or less to analyze before and after shock delivery.
- Be virtually maintenance free for a minimum of 4-5 years.

As part of purchasing an AED, a defibrillation program / protocol must be implemented – in other words an " Action Plan". Practice drills should be done once every 3-6 months for a cardiac emergency. It should be mandatory for all teachers, facilities staff and coaches to be CPR/AED certified. Offer and encourage CPR and AED training for students, parents and community members.

Education and placement of AED's has been shown to increase survival rates by 50% or more. For further information on AED's you can visit our websites at: www.NoInjury.com or www.ipsm.org. You may also go to www.early-defib.org or contact your local American Red Cross.

An example of the power of this recommendation is illustrated below:

In May of 2001, I was contacted by the producers of The Oprah Winfrey Show to co-host a segment of The Oprah Winfrey Show on the epidemic of injury in our country. Ms. Winfrey was extremely generous and kind in introducing this book, *The Awakening of a Surgeon*, to the public. In addition, she brought to the forefront the information in this book on how to make every family in our country and throughout the world safer and healthier.

On one of the segments of her show, we discussed the issue of chest impact injuries and fatalities. We discussed that if this scenario occurs, the most effective action anyone can take is to use an AED to save another's life.

Two weeks after the show aired, a 13 year-old boy in the suburbs of Chicago was struck in the chest by a baseball and went down. He was fortunate, in that, two trained physicians were in the crowd and immediately ran out to give him CPR. CPR as we have discussed is very important, but it is not enough. As they continued to give him CPR his respirations continued to decrease. At that point a **mom** in the crowd got on her cell phone and called 911. She called 911 because she knew the police officers in her community carried defibrillators in their cars.

The police officer arrived with the AED and shocked the 13 year-old boy's chest and he survived the chest impact event. When the press spoke to the mom afterwards and revealed to her that the two trained physicians did not know that an AED would save someone's life from this scenario, "how in the world did she?" Her response, "I saw it on TV. I saw it on TV." The only television show which highlighted the AED was The Oprah Winfrey Show. That **mom** in the suburbs of Chicago became empowered by Oprah Winfrey and her show. She was empowered by our information that we have included in this book to help you, your family, and your community. Unfortunately, we are continually told that one person cannot make a difference. This is just one small example of how one person can become empowered with the information that we have provided in this book, and make a positive difference.

APPENDIX FIVE

Preventing Winter Sports Injuries

The American Academy of Orthopedic Surgeons and The Institute for Preventative Sports Medicine, over the past several years, have been in partnership in developing various recommendations to the public as it relates to winter related injuries. Some of the most popular winter sports leading to injuries include **skiing**, which will lead over eighty-three thousand individuals to seek medical treatment this coming year; **hockey**, over sixty-two thousand individuals will be injured; **snowboarding**, over thirty seven thousand individuals and **sledding** over twenty-five thousand individuals injured. The total number of people injured per year, secondary to winter sports, are over **two hundred seventy thousand**. These figures include only emergency room visits and do not include non- hospitalization physician visits. Therefore, these two hundred and seventy thousand individuals are just the tip of the injury iceberg. Total healthcare costs for these injuries, including medical, legal, and other expenses, will exceed two billion dollars this year alone. Below are the recommendations developed by The American Academy of Orthopedic Surgeons in conjunction with

The Institute for Preventative Sports Medicine to prevent winter sports injuries.

General—Recommendations for safe winter sports include: 1) Conditioning off-season. 2) Buying and maintaining well-fitted equipment. 3) Warming up before all activities. 4) Resting when fatigued because the vast majority of injuries are sustained when the individual has been participating in the activity for an extended period of time. 5) Abiding by all rules and markings whether they are on the slopes or the ice rink. 6) Making sure that all participants are adequately hydrated. We tend to think of dehydration in the summer months but dehydration can also occur in the winter months with strenuous activities.

Skiing—Recommendations that have been developed thru the Academy, as well as thru the Institute, include: 1) Skiers should buy boots and bindings that have been set, adjusted and maintained by recommendations by the American Society of Testing Materials. 2) Skiers should check the binding of each ski before skiing. The binding should be adjusted based on the skier's height and weight. 3) At the start of each new ski day warm up activities and several slow runs should be accomplished before the more vigorous runs are attempted. 4) Skiers should stay at all times on marked trails. 5) Skiers should ski with partners and stay within sight of each other. 6) Skiers should rest when fatigued. 7) All skiers should wear helmets at all times. Sony Bono is a testament to the fact that no matter how advanced the skier, impact can occur with other individuals or with stationary objects such as trees or rocks, and a helmet can prevent a catastrophic head injury. 8) Carry a cell phone for emergency purposes.

Hockey—Recommendations developed thru the Academy and the Institute consist of wearing protective equipment such as: 1) Helmet and a full-face shield at all levels of play. 2) Shoulder pads. 3) Shin pads. 4) Elbow pads. 5) Hip pads. 6) Gloves. 7) Mouth guard. 8)Eyeglasses, if worn, are to be made of non-shattered glass. 9) No head checking at all levels of play.

Cross Country Skiing—The vast majority of injuries are due to overuse. Therefore, an adequate warm up and conditioning program is of paramount importance in preventing cross-country skiing injuries.

Sledding—The vast majority of sledding injuries are related to impact and the inadequate use of the sled itself. Recommendations include: 1) All participants must sit in a forward facing position steering with their feet or a rope tied to the steering handles of the sled. 2) No one should sled head first down a slope. 3) A helmet should be worn by all individuals sledding. 4) No one should sled on slopes that end in a street, parking lot, or body of water. 5) Do not slide on plastic sheets or other materials that can be pierced by a stick or a rock that can lead to significant injury.

Hydration—With all winter sports remember to push fluids before, during and after activities in order to avoid dehydration.

Swimming and Water Safety

One thousand children will drown this year in the United States and **three thousand children** will experience near drowning events this coming year as well. The good news is the vast majority, if not the entirety, of the drownings and near drownings are completely preventable with the points listed below.

- Adult supervision is needed at all times for swimming pool, lake, and river activity.

- All adults and teenagers should be knowledgeable and proficient in CPR (Cardio Pulmonary Resuscitation).

- Never swim alone or in unsupervised areas.

- Avoid the dangerous TOOS: Too Tired, Too Cold, and Too Far From Safety.

- No alcohol should be consumed before or during water activities.

- All children age 4 years of age or older should be enrolled in swim classes.

- Do not use water wings in place of life jackets.

- Check the weather report before any water activities.

- Nine feet of water is needed as a minimum depth for diving activities.

POOL SAFETY

The above listed prevention steps should also be utilized for pool safety as well as:

- A fence must be installed at least 4 feet in height, which has a self-closing and self-latching gate.

- Floating alarms in the pool should be utilized at all times in case a child happens to fall into a pool.

- Arm Band alarms may also be utilized on each child to prevent a drowning or near drowning.

- Cell phones should be available at all times

- Make sure pool has dual drains and intact drain covers to prevent hair entanglement and body part entrapment.

- Make sure parents, lifeguards and/or staff know where, and can access, the pump power cut-off switch is so that it can be turned off in an emergency.

Playground Safety

Over Five-hundred thousand children will be injured in playgrounds in the United States this year alone. The vast majority of these injuries are completely preventable. Of the children injured in playgrounds, 58% of all injuries to children will be due to a fall on a **hard surface.** The following prevention points, if implemented, would drastically reduce the occurrence of playground injuries:

Surface

- Create a softer surface such as a surface made of wood mulch, shredded tires, or sand at least 1 foot in thickness. Surfaces such as asphalt, concrete, hard packed dirt, or grass are not sufficient in order to prevent injury.

Design

- Separate active play areas for swinging and jumping vs. quiet play areas such as sand boxes.

- Separate play areas for younger vs. older children.

- Use zones should be created to avoid collisions.

- Barriers between play areas and streets should be created with fences.

Maintenance

- Equipment should be made of durable materials free from sharp edges, rust, exposed or loose screws or nails.

- The drop and watch technique vs. the drop and run technique is preferable.

- Bringing a book, laptop computer or paperwork to keep the adult at the playground area so that a semi-supervised or supervised environment can be created for the health and welfare of each child in the playground area.

The Pre-Participation Physical Exam

The purpose of the pre-participation physical exam is to drastically reduce the occurrence of sudden cardiac death in sports. The two most common causes of sudden cardiac death are: a thickening of the muscle of the heart and abnormalities of the arteries supplying blood to the heart. It has been estimated that 1 in 500 athletes have a thickening of the heart muscle.

On average 6-20% of athletes will require further evaluation based on their exam and 2% of athletes will be disqualified from participation. This exam is mandatory for every person in every age group who will be participating in a sports activity.

An important component of the exam is a careful medical history focusing on the symptoms of: chest pain, palpitations, passing out with exertion, light-headedness, murmur, and a positive family history. An annual history and physical exam should occur at least −6 weeks prior to the start of an athletic season. Unfortunately, the usual scenario is to wait until the last minute and rush to turn in the paperwork. Time must be given in order to allow further testing in case positive findings are discovered at the initial evaluation.

In addition to a through history the major components of the exam consist of: pulse-rate and regularity, blood pressure, and listening to the heart and lungs with a stethoscope.

With the above steps the incidence of sudden cardiac death can be significantly reduced.

Preventing Baseball and Softball Injuries

- Certified Coach knowledgeable in baseball/softball conditioning and training.
- AED at the field.
- Coach knowledgeable and proficient in CPR and AED use.
- Field equipped with break-away bases.
- Lighter weight baseballs for the youngest players.
- Stretching and warm up period prior to play and stretching and cool down periods after play.
- Unlimited quantity of water available.
- Helmets for batters, runners and catchers.
- Well groomed field without potholes.
- Padded fences.
- No one should swing a bat other than in the on-deck circle or at the plate.
- Face shields on all helmets.
- Only one ball in play at a time (infield practice should not occur at the same time as batting practice on the same field).

Preventing Soccer Injuries

- Certified Coach knowledgeable in soccer conditioning and training.

- AED at the field.

- Coach knowledgeable and proficient in CPR and AED use.

- Field equipped with goal posts that are stationary to the ground to prevent tip over injuries. The post must also be padded.

- Shin Guards that use air-padding systems.

- Stretching and warm up period prior to play and stretching and cool down period after play.

- Unlimited quantity of water available.

- Well groomed field without potholes.

- Proper heading techniques in practices should be taught utilizing a lightweight beach ball to minimize the concussive effect of a standard soccer ball.

APPENDIX ELEVEN

The Six Sigma Approach

The Institute for Preventative Sports Medicine has utilized the Six Sigma Approach in our efforts to reduce injuries in sport. This same approach that we have utilized can be applied to solving issues related to cancer, heart disease, obesity, terrorism and for that matter any potential issue at hand.

The Institute's application of the Six Sigma Approach includes:

- Define the Issue
- Measure the Issue
- Analyze the Issue
- Improve the Issue
- Control the Issue

With application of these five steps we have found that the vast majority of injuries can be prevented. It is also our contention that the vast majority of issues at hand in healthcare, and outside of healthcare, could drastically be diminished, if not eliminated.

The Politics of Prevention- Breaking Down the Barriers

David H. Janda, M.D.

It has been said by individuals within the mass media that each and every American will remember where they were and what they were doing on September 11th 2001. It has been said we will remember that day, that awful day, just as we had the day the Challenger blew up, the day John F. Kennedy was assassinated, and the day Pearl Harbor was bombed. Whenever a horrible event occurs, I immediately think of the words of wisdom from my father, " Things always happen for a reason and they always work out for the best in the long run." On countless occasions, whether it has been a personal tragedy, or a tragedy experienced by our society, I am always confident, at the time, that he will be proven wrong. To date his philosophy has always won out over fear, anger, and at times hopelessness. Just as we triumphed after these other disasters, I believe, that every citizen, every family, and our entire country will grow because of what happened to the over 3,000 that were killed needlessly and the 7,000 that were injured.

As parents, grandparents, community activists and community leaders, we need to search for lessons from this horrible experience. Within two days after the collapse of the World Trade Center and the destruction of the Pentagon, I received several calls from throughout the United States of individuals wanting to talk to me about the philosophy that I put forward in my book, *The Awakening of a Surgeon*. These individuals called to tell me that they utilized our preventive approach in trying to make sense out of the mayhem. The callers suggested that I immediately get in touch with individuals within government and help educate them on how to become proactive rather than reactive so that disasters of this nature never occur again. The callers felt that if government officials thought in a more proactive or preventive manner, such as we have done in the Sports Medicine world, that possibly our country and our world would become a safer place.

Needless to say, I could not agree more. The politics of prevention and the barriers to preventive efforts whether it is in sports medicine, heart disease, cancer, or terrorism are similar. Over the past seventeen years, I have found that **the single greatest barrier to preventive efforts is the fact that we are taught throughout our educational system to be reactive rather than being proactive**. To think in a proactive or preventative manner is a much different mindset than thinking in a reactive mindset. It involves a different set of observation skills and a different set of implementation skills. Unfortunately, from kindergarten through graduate school reactive thought is the norm and preventative thought is completely ignored. In my own case, the use of a proactive thought process was integrated in my family life and not taught in any of my schooling throughout grammar school, high school, college, medical school or residency. I believe, as parents, grandparents, community leaders and activists, we owe it to those around us, no matter what the age, to start to integrate proactive and preventative measures and thought in our daily teachings rather than purely a reactionary philosophy and thought processes.

The second barrier that we have faced dealing with preventive intervention is that the status quo carries with it great momentum. We have a saying at The Institute for Preventative Sports Medicine that "When it comes to prevention, caring is the first step, but for it to be more than empty rhetoric action must follow." The operative word in this statement is action. Unfortunately, it is much easier to sit by and let the world pass us by and then react as opposed to being proactive in order to prevent a sports injury, cardiac disease, cancer or for that matter terrorism. It is much easier to let the world shape us rather than let us shape the world.

The third barrier to preventative intervention focuses on financial issues. In many instances the financial powers that be are ingrained in the status quo, and ingrained in reactionary behavior, and have no financial interest in preventive interventions. Therefore, preventive interventions die on the vine because there are no financial incentives for them to grow and take shape. We have found immense pressure against our preventive interventions as I point out in the book by large financial interests, including insurance companies, HMO's, government officials, the sports equipment industry, and leaders within youth and adult sports that have a vested financial interest in the status quo. Unfortunately, in order to move the ball down the field in the preventive world, one has to take on these vested financial interests. Unfortunately, many are not willing to do so, many are afraid to do so, and many just don't want to expend the energy to do so. I believe as parents, grandparents, community activists and leaders we owe it to our country and to our children to take on these financial interests. We must put aside our own fears and become involved. If we fail to do so, we are our own terrorists and our own way of life will be forever altered.

In our country, 140,000 Americans will die this year because of unintentional injury. Injuries that are sustained in motor vehicle events, unintentional firearm injuries, and sports and recreation injuries. Sixty-two million Americans will seek health care for unintentional injuries this year alone. The vast majority of which are preventable. Just as we have awakened to the terrorists on and off our own shores who perpetrated their heinous acts on September, 11, 2001, we need to awaken to the terrorist of injury which leads to needles loss of life, pain, suffering and life long disability. Injury transcends gender, race, nationality, age, and continental divides and shelves. **Twelve million student athletes between ages 5 and 22 will sustain a sport or recreational injury this year alone and will miss twenty million days of school, the vast majority of which are completely preventable.**

I believe, if we collectively utilize preventative methods, we could vastly reduce, if not completely eliminate, the issue of injury in our society. I also believe if we utilize those same techniques, we could drastically reduce cardiac disease, cancer, and even terrorism. As I point out in *The Awakening of a Surgeon*, there are various methods that each and every parent can implement in our home life in order to reduce the risk and severity of injuries. I also believe we should utilize these same techniques and same proactive thought processes in eliminating terrorism from our shores.

I believe, if we utilize my father's philosophy and learn from our mistakes and utilize preventative and proactive activities, our country, our homes, our playgrounds, and our gymnasiums will all become safer from the terrorists outside of our shores and the terrorist of injury. After all, Homeland Security does not start and stop in some cave thousands of miles away. Homeland Security starts in our own backyards, neighborhoods, community and school districts.

Medical Savings Accounts –
An Idea Whose Time Has Come

BRUCE PATTERSON
7TH DISTRICT
P.O. BOX 30036
LANSING, MICHIGAN 48909-7536
PHONE: (517) 373-7350
FAX: (517) 373-9228
senbpatterson@senate.michigan.gov

THE SENATE
STATE OF
MICHIGAN

COMMITTEES:
TECHNOLOGY AND ENERGY, CHAIR
NATURAL RESOURCES AND
ENVIRONMENTAL AFFAIRS, VICE CHAIR
MEMBER:
HEALTH POLICY JUDICIARY

For Immediate Release
January 30, 2004

Contact: Bob Mauseth
517-373-7350

Patterson bills establish Medical savings accounts
Plymouth surgeon and author key to legislative package

Lansing – Income tax deductions for preventative health care services will be available and a new medical savings account will be created under a package of bills being introduced next week by Sen. Bruce Patterson (R-Canton).

In addition, the bills will allow for a Single Business Tax or Income Tax credit for contributions to a medical savings account.

"It's time to put the power for health care where it belongs, in the hands of the people," Patterson said. "Lives will be saved when people know they can use tax-deferred funds for preventative measures such as mammograms, well-baby checks, and annual physicals."

Senator Patterson serves as Vice-Chair of the Michigan Senate Health Policy Committee. His constituent, Dr. David Janda of Plymouth, Michigan, is the author of <u>Awakening of a Surgeon</u>. According to Patterson, this book and conversations with Dr. Janda have been instrumental in the development of this legislative package and his work on the committee. "Dr. Janda and colleagues like him are a testament to their profession," said Patterson. "He has identified a problem, researched it, and offered a solution. I look forward to the consideration of this approach by the Michigan Senate and I'm proud to offer it to my colleagues."

Dr. David Janda is encouraged by the response of his own state Senator. "Senator Patterson has taken my work to heart," said Janda. "Medical savings accounts will change lives as people take control of their health care and how they get it. As our population ages, the cost of health care increases. This is an important way we can help control costs and make people safer and healthier."

A Celebration of the life of Benjamin H. Janda

. . . This edition is dedicated to my father, Benjamin H. Janda, who passed away suddenly but peacefully on January 28, 2003. I was given the opportunity of delivering my father's eulogy on Saturday, February 1, 2003. At the conclusion of the eulogy a number of people asked that I put down in writing the words of tribute that I gave to my father. This presentation is a celebration of the life of my dad and his philosophies of life from which all of us can benefit.

—David H. Janda, M.D.

The Celebration

. . . I would like to thank each and every one of you for taking the time from your day to join us. It is an extremely sad occasion in the Janda Family, but by being here you are honoring both my mom and my dad. One of the first lessons I received at the Ben and Ruth Janda School of Higher Education was that the single greatest gift you can give to someone or something is **your time and your efforts**. By being here today, you are giving your time to our family. On behalf of each and every member of the Janda Family, I would like to thank you for making the effort to join us in honor of my father, Benjamin H. Janda.

Over the years, I have had the fortunate opportunity of giving hundreds of presentations around the world, but this by far is the hardest and the most important presentation I will ever give. In one of my early discussions with my father we discussed the issue of adulthood. He mentioned to me that one doesn't become an adult at fifteen years of age when one gets ones drivers permit, or at twenty-one years of age when one can legally drink, or at eighteen years of age when someone becomes eligible for the draft. He once told me that one becomes an adult when your first parent dies. I am now four days into adulthood and can easily say I don't like it and I surely wish I could return to the pre-adolescent years of my life.

Over the past four days, there is one word that keeps surfacing in the description of my Dad. The word is **saint**. On Tuesday night, when I came back home to Chicago, and I started to make phone calls to the friends and acquaintances of the Janda Family, of the first sixty phone calls I made, one of the first statements repeatedly made was "You know Dave, your dad was a Saint!" The next day, when I went to the post office to drop off some mail the postal clerks started to cry when they heard "Saint Ben had died." When I went to the dry cleaner the woman at the counter started to weep and cry when she heard of the passing of my dad, "Saint Ben." When I picked up prescriptions at the local pharmacy, the pharmacist bowed his head in silence and was visibly moved upon hearing of the death of my dad. The waitress that usually served my parents at one of their favorite restaurants was also visibly moved and told me the story that "Saint Ben" knew that she was a single mom and every time he came in he would tip her forty percent and before he left the restaurant he would take another twenty dollars and put it in her hand and say "This is for your eleven year old boy." The fact that my father was a Saint was, as he would say, " No new news", at least to me. What amazed me was how many other people also realized that my father was truly a Saint. You see, in my life, I have truly been blessed because there are five Saints in my life that have helped me down the road and continue to help me. I essentially just go along for the ride. The saints in my life have been my dad and my mom, my wife, Libby, and our two beautiful daughters, Allison and Katie. I have truly won the lottery when it comes to being surrounded by Saints.

In addition to being a Saint, my father was my **idol**. He has been my idol for the past forty-four years and will continue to be my idol every day for the rest of my life. There are two mementos that I would like to share with you about my father. Both are books. Both were dedicated to him. One at the beginning of his life, and one in the twilight years of his life.

The first memento was written to my father, and about my father, by his "favorite aunt", Ella. In this hand written book she detailed the birth and the early years of Ben Janda's life.

On November 12, 1920, at 8:00 p.m., a baby boy weighing 8 pounds saluted his way into the world in Chicago, Illinois. It was decided that the "little fellow" would be named Benjamin Hubert Janda. Benjamin, in honor of the attending physician who patiently and diligently harbored this grand baby boy into a new world. The physician's name was Dr. Benjamin D. Satek, an uncle to little Benjamin's mother, Mae Kleisner Janda. The middle name honors are credited to the proud father, Hubert J. Janda.

Everyone loved the new baby because he was "cute" and well-behaved. His crying was very limited. Each day Benjamin grew, he was loved more and more by his parents and grandparents, uncles and aunts, especially Ella (A little bit of marketing by Ella). He soon was called "Sunny" because he possessed a sunny disposition. His beautiful dimpled smile and outstanding personality won him many admiring glances and praises.

. . . The best way I can describe my father is as a fine piece of Bohemian Crystal. You see, Czechoslovakia and Bohemia are well known for their beautiful Crystal with their many facets. My father was like a fine piece of Bohemian Crystal with so many facets. Each one of those facets representing the loves of his life. God was kind to my father and shone light on him every single day of his life. When that light struck him it exploded off of him in a multitude of colors shining and helping everyone and everything around him. As I mentioned, each one of the intricate facets of my father were in fact, each one of his loves. He loved being a great son and nephew. He dedicated his life to the health and well being of his parents, his aunts, and his uncles. Every weekend, for years on end he would drop everything he was doing and visit either his aunts or his uncles in various locations throughout the city of Chicago. He always had time for his elders and in fact, he brought his own mom, my grandmother, into our home for a number of years until her death.

. . . He loved being a great husband. My mother and my father truly have been outstanding role models for myself, my friends and other members of our family about what a great marriage can be. They truly have been partners in life and will continue to be partners from this point on in a different realm. I can honestly say, I never heard my parents yell at each other or fight. In addition, a number of my friends and people in their current neighborhood, have said they have tried to model their marriages after my parents. They are both very giving individuals, very tolerant individuals and always willing to go the extra mile for each other. They truly have been great role models for all of us.

My father loved being a great father. No matter how busy he was at work he always had time for his son. We spoke 3-4 times a week on the phone. We communicated by mail another 3-4 times every week for our entire lives since we have been apart when I went to college. He always attended any game I participated in. Any time I was on TV or radio, he always made the extra effort to watch or listen. But, what I remember most of my dad in the early years, was him always being willing to give me time after a long day at work. In the early years, my father would work fourteen to sixteen hours a day. When he would return home late at night he always had time to play catch with me. You see, my dad was a great baseball player in high school and college. He in turn helped me become a very good player throughout high school. It started early in life with him taking the time to play catch. Every night he'd come home and as he sat down to dinner I would start to get our gloves and ball ready so that we could play catch after dinner. Even when he came home late at night, while he ate dinner, I would set up the flashlights in the backyard so we could play catch. One particular evening after I set up the flashlights, when I was about eight, I ran downstairs to get a ball. I picked it off the top of his filing cabinet and joined him outside. Many times when we played, the only time you knew the ball was thrown at you, because it was so dark, was when the ball would hit you and would almost knock you over. It was amazing how he could so effortlessly throw a baseball, yet have it hit so hard in my glove and burn so hard in the palm of my hand. One night as we played catch I threw the ball to him. He caught it. He looked at the ball and said "Dave, we need to talk." As I came over to him he said "Dave, I didn't anticipate us talking about this at this point, but now is better than any other time. You see, this baseball you just threw to me Dave, was a ball that was given to me by my father to give to you. This ball was signed by somebody who never signed baseballs or any piece of paper for that matter, but somehow your grandfather got him to sign this ball. This ball was signed by Shoeless Joe Jackson, Dave, and this is one expensive ball. So it probably would be best that we not play with it." My father always had time for me whether I was four years old playing catch or forty-four years old just to talk. He always made time for family, friends, and above all, his son.

My father loved being a great father-in-law. He saw Libby, to his dying day, as the daughter he never had and her four sisters as the daughters he also never had. He included the Frederick Family in the Janda Family and treated them as if they were his own. One side of my father that I think very few people ever saw was his "psychic abilities." You see, the first time he met Libby we were far from ever going out. He first met Libby about a year and a half before we went out while we were both at Bucknell University. At that point my parents were having dinner with former President Ford and the President of Bucknell University and his wife. Libby used to work in the restaurant associated with the University. Libby happened to serve my parents and former President Ford and the President of the University and his wife dinner. At one point in the meal my father turned to my mother and said "Ruth, do you know who that girl is?" My mom said "No, she seems very pleasant but I don't know who she is." My dad looked at her and said "Ruth, that's your future daughter-in-law." With that President Ford looked at my father and said " Oh, your son goes out with her." My dad looked at President Ford and said "No, not yet. He doesn't know it yet, but they're going to get married." My mom and my dad never told me that story until the day Libby and I got married.

My father loved being a grandfather. He taught my daughters the finer points of how to win at The Wheel of Fortune and how to bet pennies on football games. He loved getting them quarters with the states on them to collect and he loved going to their various types of games. They truly were the apples of his eye. Earlier Libby, in her tribute to my father, mentioned that so much of my dad is present in our daughters. One of the traits that my daughters inherited from my father was a streak of bull headedness. What truly amazes me is how that trait skipped a generation. My father was, is, and will always be so very proud of his granddaughters who have grown up to be such wonderful, caring, and giving individuals.

. . . My father loved being, and was, a great engineer and a great businessman. My father built a company, A. L Jackson, and built their reputation to heights that the Jackson Company could never have imagined. My father was famous in our family for the quote "When you're given a load of lemons, make lemonade." In other words, from bad times can come better times if you make the effort. My father was handed a Lindahl size truck full of lemons in his career. You see, the Jackson Family had promised my father that when the Jackson Family would step away from the construction company, my father would take over the reins of the company. It just so happened that the Jackson Family sold the company out from under my father and in a word—screwed him. But my father, rather that shriveling up and curling up in a little ball and withering away, decided to make lemonade out of lemons. He founded B.H. Janda Construction Incorporated, which initially started building commercial garages. He built that business into a business that led to a significant enhancement of the Chicago skyline. His company worked on the John Hancock Building, the C.N.A. Building, the corporate head quarters for AT&T, Ameritech, United Airlines, the Chicago Filtration Plant, and built a portion of O'Hare International Airport. When my grandmother died, Mayor Daley, *the Mayor Daley*, attended the wake. At one point at the wake Mayor Daley approached me and looked at me and said "Are you Ben Janda's kid?" I was little, and I looked up at him and said "Yes Sir, I am." His response was "Do you know that your father is the only person who ever told me to go to hell and got away with it? You see the reason I let him get away with it is because your father is one of the most honest people I know. When your father told me to go to hell I had that coming, because your father was honest enough with me to tell me things I needed to know, and they were things I didn't want to hear. The best thing you can do, David, is be like your father, and if you do you will become a great person."

At one time I asked my father what the greatest accomplishment was in his business career. Was it the Hancock Building? The CNA Building? The US Steel Plant in Gary? Was it the Filtration Plant? What was it? He looked at me and said " My greatest accomplishment, Dave, was bringing together a group of people that I loved and who in return, loved me back." Those people, were responsible, not just one person, but all of us were responsible for working together and building structures that will last for centuries. You see, it was the people that were my father's greatest accomplishment. One of the things he did was that every year he would put money aside, without telling his employees, for each one of them. When they retired, he, in a room by themselves, would present the money to each one of his workers for all their efforts in helping the company. Each one of those workers retired so that they did not have any further financial worries for the rest of their lives. Contrast this to what we are seeing with Enron and some of these other companies that will do anything in their power to steal from their employees rather than help their employees. All of the people in corporate America could learn something from my father.

. . . My father loved sports and he loved being an athlete. My father was a great pitcher in high school and college. He threw many, many no hitters in his favorite sport, baseball. He used to say "Sports do not build character, they reveal it." He turned his interest in baseball, into my interest in baseball. At one point in my career I became a very good baseball pitcher in high school. I never threw a no hitter but, I threw a number of one hitters and two hitters. On one particular day I threw a three hitter as a pitcher and at the plate I went three for four. I hit two grand slam home runs and hit a double with two men on base and had ten RBI's. However, my third time up at bat I grounded to the short stop with men on second and third and ended the inning. At the end of the game when I came out of the dugout, there was my dad there to hug me and to congratulate me. He congratulated me on a "great game" and then he asked "So Dave, What are you going to remember about today's game?" I said, " What I am going to remember most is when I hit that second grand slam home run the outfielder threw his glove on the ground when the ball went over the wall." He looked at me and said " Dave, That will be a great memory, but what I also want you to remember is how it felt when you grounded out to the short-stop with men on second and third." You see, this was time for another one of Ben's life lessons. He said "If you only remember your successes in life you will never grow, you will never improve, you always must remember your successes but, you must also must remember when you come up short because that is the only way you will become better whether it is baseball or whatever you might choose in life." When it came to any sport he always transcended that sport into a higher meaning in life.

He loved to bowl and used to bowl on a league every Thursday night with his buddies that he had since high school and college. Occasionally, when I didn't have school on Fridays, I would substitute in that league. It was funny that when everyone else bought drinks they would only buy drinks for their team. Yet, when my dad bought drinks, he'd buy drinks for his team and also the team they were bowling against. One time I asked my father "Dad, why do you spend all this extra money buying drinks for the other team." He said to me, "Dave, whatever you are dealing with, whenever you have an adversary, treat them honestly and fairly as though you would want them to treat you, because when it all comes down, win or lose, you can look at the other side and say, I gave you every chance to succeed and either you did or you didn't. If your opponents are on their A-game they'll make you perform to your A-game."

He also enjoyed to golf. He used to hit the ball a tremendous distance, further than anyone I've seen, but it was never straight. He would go up to the tee, pull his driver out, hit a ball screaming down the fairway only to have it keep curving right, and right, and further right. When it would land he'd turn around and look at me and go "Just off the fairway" and I'd say "Dad, you are way off the fairway!" and he would say "Dave, I'm just off the fairway, two fairways over." As we'd walk to the ball my dad once said to me, "Dave, I think you don't really understand this game. You shoot a great game of golf and you are always in the middle of the fairway, but, golf is not about how you are shooting, or how you are playing, it's about who you are playing with. Today it's 75 and sunny and I am playing with my son and my wife, we are on the third hole and as far as I'm concerned, I am ten under par."

My father loved being a great friend. Libby, in her tribute to my father, mentioned a number of my dad's friends. But one friend Libby is completely unaware of is a fellow by the name of Hank Vilotel. Hank was a genius. My father grew up with Hank. Hank never got married and he took care of his mother till her dying days. When we would get done bowling on Thursday night we would stop off at a coffee shop to have a hamburger and fries with Hank. Hank was a loner, but one night as we sat eating our hamburger and fries, Hank was visibly upset. Hank looked at my dad and said, "Ben, I went to the doctor yesterday. I've been told I have bone marrow cancer and I am dying." My father's jaw fell open. Hank then said, "Ben, I need your help." My father immediately responded "Anything and everything Hank." Hank then produced a number of papers. He said, "Ben, Fifty other people that I was in my military division with died of the same thing, and there are another forty that are sick with the same ailment. Ben, I believe we were exposed to nuclear radiation in the desserts of Nevada and that's why we are all dying of bone marrow cancer." He said, "Ben, I don't know anybody as honest as you, and as tenacious as you, that could possibly help." My dad took the papers, read the papers, and then contacted people he knew in Washington in order to get reparations for all of the servicemen and their families, that succumbed to radiation disease from being exposed to test nuclear explosions in the deserts of Nevada.

My father was a great soldier and a great patriot. He loved being a soldier and a patriot. As was pointed out in Ella's comments, when my father was born, he was born saluting. I always thought that this was a fictitious claim until I talked to my grandmother who said, "David, trust me, I was part of the process, I can still remember the pain, Yes, your father was born saluting." When my mom called me and told me of the severe trouble my father was in Tuesday morning. One of the first things that popped into my mind was him being a soldier. When he was brought into this world saluting, my goal was that when he left this world someone salute him. When I once asked him what his worst days were in his life I thought surely he would say when he was in the military and going across the northern Atlantic in Liberty ships going to England and then going to other locations in Europe to fight. He said to me, "No Dave, my worst day was not the days of being involved in any type of combat activity. My worst day is an easy one, it was the day my dad died." I can surely tell you that the worst day in my life was January 28, 2003. But, on that day, I went back to an old statement. A statement that I have used hundreds of times, "What would my dad do?" When I got home on Tuesday, I called several friends of mine in the military. One of the friends I called was in the Pentagon and he helped arrange a flag for my father, and an honor guard for his funeral. I believe that he came into this world saluting, and when he was going to leave this world someone was going to salute him.

The second memento I have, is a book I had something to do with. The book I wrote, *The Awakening of a Surgeon*. **The book is about perseverance, dedication and sacrifice to others**. It is what my parents are about. It is how they have lived their lives and what they have tried to instill in their son. The book was dedicated to my father, as well as my mom, my wife, and our children. As I pointed out in the dedication, my parents taught me to keep my feet on the ground and reach for the stars. I have truly had the fortunate opportunity to grasp onto three shining stars, my wife and my two daughters, who truly are the personification of what my father was and is about. I was also gratified when my dad used to keep telling me how he kept reading the book, and how he enjoyed the book. One of the parts I believe he enjoyed was in the introduction where I point out that the foundation and superstructure of the book, and the efforts behind it, all emanated from my family. My parents, Ben and Ruth Janda, my wife, Libby, and our two beautiful daughters, Allison and Katie, are the inspiration and driving force of my life, my efforts, and this book. The "Janda Fab Five" have guided and counseled me throughout my journey. Without their help, and support, my efforts would have been for naught. I truly have been blessed to have them as a part of my life and as my best friends. That book, about a year and a half ago, was featured on the Oprah Winfrey Show. I was asked to co-host the show with Oprah. As I sat next to Oprah she said to me, "I understand your family is in the audience." I said, "Yes, they are Oprah. My mom and my dad, my wife, my children, my aunts and some friends are all here." She said, "Point them out to me." As I pointed them out I realized that they all looked incredibly scared and petrified. Oprah said to me, " They look a little afraid." I said, "Oprah, they look a lot afraid." And, as we went down the row and I pointed out to her who everyone was, we came to my dad and he was leaning forward in his seat and Oprah said to me, "Who is that guy with the huge smile?" I said "Oprah, that's my dad!" When I said that to her, in true Ben fashion, he raised his cane, swung it around in the air, and then mouthed the words to me, "Give'em hell Dave!" You see, whenever my father faced a challenge he saw it as an opportunity, an opportunity to make a difference. He instilled that in me. "Put fear aside Dave, seize the moment, make a difference" was another of Ben's life lessons.

As I mentioned earlier, my father was a huge baseball fan. He played in high school and college at a high level and he did extremely well. He took me to my first baseball game at two months of age and to numerous baseball games throughout my life. I also watched many games with him on TV and listened to many games on the radio with him. The past several years however, one of the things we did when he visited our house was that we would watch baseball movies. One of the individuals on our Advisory Board at the Institute, whose name is Bill Kinsella, wrote a book *Shoeless Joe Jackson*, about the same fellow who signed that baseball that my dad and I played catch with. That book, *Shoeless Joe Jackson*, was made into the movie, *Field of Dreams*. I bought the movie for dad and we watched it. At one point in the movie I heard my dad crying. We were at the part of the movie where the main character, Kevin Costner, plays catch with his father who comes out of the corn field. I looked at my dad because this was so unlike him to be crying like this. I said, "Dad, what is wrong!" and he said "Dave, I love life and love everything in life, but what I miss most in life is playing catch with my dad." You see this past Tuesday, January 28, 2003, was a devastating day for the Janda Family. It was what September 11th was to our country. Our skyscraper, our World Trade Center, collapsed in our home. However, on Tuesday morning, January 28th I feel something very special happened in our house. You see my mom was in the house, my dad was in the house, and God sent my father's father to our house with two gloves and a ball. And when my father died, he died playing catch with his father. This can only explain how he passed so peacefully, so effortlessly, and with a smile on his face. My father fought every day of his life to do good, to move the ball down the field. But on that day, God presented him an opportunity that he had missed for many years and he graciously accepted it.

His death was not the first time I experienced death in our family. The first time I experienced death was when my Uncle Frank died. I was about six years of age. I remember that day very vividly. Every night my father and I at eight o'clock at night would go to the local newsstand and get two Chicago Tribunes. One for my dad, and one for his Aunt Jo, who lived three blocks from us. Aunt Jo taught my father how to read. She also taught me how to read. Every night we'd go to her house and deliver the paper. That night she was sobbing because her youngest brother had died. As she cried my dad hugged her and consoled her, and as he left he said his usual farewell, "Dobra Naughts." Dobra Naughts in Czechoslovakian means, "good-bye until we see each other again." As we walked hand in hand down the sidewalk from Aunt Jo's house to our car I said to my dad, "What are you going to say to Uncle Frank tomorrow when he gets buried?" My dad said, "Dave, I don't know. What do you think I should say?" I said,

"Why don't you say, Dobra Naughts." He said, "I think that's really a great idea Dave, and I'm gonna do that." As we continued to walk to the car I said, "Well dad, at least I don't have to worry about that." He said, "Dave, What do you mean?" I said, "Well dad, I know you are never going to die so I'll never have to say anything." With that he stopped, he bent down on his knees and he grabbed my hands, his big brown eyes looking in mine and said, "Dave, I'm gonna die someday, you're gonna die, everyone we know is gonna die. Hopefully it will be many years in the future." And with that I asked one of those very insensitive six year-old questions. I looked at dad and said, "So dad, when you die, what do you want me to say?" and he looked at me and said, "Dave, why don't you say Dobra Naughts." With that he rose, we held hands, and we walked to the car. We then did what we did every night of the week even though, Mom, Dad told you we only did it once a month, we did it every night. He would get in the driver side. I would get into the passenger side. He would look in the rear view mirror and say, "Dave, I don't see any police, hop over." I'd get on his lap and I would take the steering wheel and he would use the accelerator and brake pedal. Usually we kept the car on the road, some nights we didn't keep it on the road accidentally, some nights actually we purposely ended up driving on lawns. But Mom, now I think I can level with you on what happened one particular night. You remember that yellow fire hydrant on the corner of 51st and Caroline? And, Mom, you remember Dad's green Chevy Impala, and Mom, I'm sure you remember that huge yellow dent in the left front fender of Dad's Impala. Well, it just so happened, Mom, that one night we got off the road and we hit the fire hydrant. And I can still remember the next day when you went out to get a paper and saw the huge yellow mark and yelled for my dad about what happened to his car and he came out and said,

"Ruth, I never realized we had vandals in the neighborhood. I'll look into it."

So, now I come to the time that I have dreaded for the past thirty-eight years, ever since my dad delivered that first lesson on death on Aunt Jo's front sidewalk. I want to thank you dad, for being a great son, nephew, brother-in-law, husband, father, father-in-law, grandfather, friend, businessman, engineer, citizen, soldier and patriot and making it all look so easy. You once told me "You know someone is good at something if they make it look easy." Dad, you made it all look easy. You taught me how to live and on Tuesday morning you taught me how to die with dignity and grace. I want to thank you for being my idol for the past forty-four years. And, I also want to thank you for continuing to be my idol every day for the rest of my life until the day you show up at my house, hopefully many decades from now, with two gloves and a ball.

"I love you Dad. I will always love you Dad, Dobra Naughts"

ORDER FORM ~ *The Awakening of a Surgeon*

Please enclose this postcard with payment

Total quantity _____ x $12.95 = _____

Shipping & Handling _____

Shipping & Handling: USA orders – ($4 first book /$3 each additional)
International Orders – (add $6 per book for S&H)

TOTAL: $ _____

☐ Yes, please have book signed and personalized by Dr. Janda To: _____

Payment Method:

☐ check or money order *(made payable to: I.P.S.M.)*

☐ VISA ☐ MC Credit Card # _____

Exp. date _____ Signature _____

Send payment and order to:
I.P.S.M.
P.O. Box 7032
Ann Arbor, MI 48107
USA

You may also order by faxing:
(734) 572-4503

SHIPPING INFORMATION

Name _____

Address _____

City/State/Zip _____

Phone (___) _____ email _____

DAVID H. JANDA, MD

The AWAKENING *of a* SURGEON

A Family Guide to Preventing Sports Injuries and Death

The Institute for Preventative Sports Medicine
P.O. Box 7032
Ann Arbor, MI 48107

Affix
Postage
Here